BEYOND *the* GARDEN

BEYOND *the* GARDEN

Designing Home Landscapes with Natural Systems

Dana Davidsen

PRINCETON ARCHITECTURAL PRESS · NEW YORK

TABLE OF CONTENTS

Introduction:
A Call to Coauthorship

TIMOTHY A. SCHULER

A ll landscapes are authored. Places we call "natural" do not persist in some eternal state of being. They have been written into existence by atmospheric, biological, and gravitational forces. They are the product of heaving tectonics, pioneering seeds, and the scouring properties of wind and rain. Increasingly, however, coauthorship belongs to us. The landscape you see outside your window is the result of climatic factors as well as economic policy, commercial exploration, and aesthetic preference. In a word, society. As Jedediah Purdy, law professor and author of *This Land Is Our Land: The Struggle for a New Commonwealth* and *After Nature: A Politics for the Anthropocene*, has written, civilization itself is a kind of "collective landscape architecture." We make the world through the act of living.

Growing up in rural Kansas, I gained an early understanding of how modern society could rewrite the landscape—for both good and ill. What once was fertile tallgrass prairie had, over the course of 150 years, been cleared, graded, and ploughed into a rigid checkerboard of gravel roads and agricultural fields, with entire cultures and ecosystems displaced in the process. Rivers were dammed, levees built. In the western part of the state, where my grandparents farmed, oil and water wells punctured the earth, the landscape disfigured by mechanical pumpjacks and robot-like center-pivot irrigation systems.

My family lived outside of a small town in eastern Kansas on twenty-six acres of former farmland. On it was a barn, a granary, two silos, a maze of corrals for livestock, a stone storm cellar, and a small, ranch-style house. The house was nondescript, with peeling green paint, beige brick, and a jagged fault line running through the middle of its concrete porch. The outbuildings and corrals were rusted, and the flagstones in the north patio popped up at odd angles.

The landscape, on the other hand, was full of life and care. Behind the house was a fifteen-hundred-square-foot garden that every summer produced sweet corn, potatoes, spinach, melons, tomatoes, and more. Around the house, my mother, a landscape designer, filled planting beds with her favorite flowers, especially bright-colored, trumpet-shaped blooms that brought hordes of hummingbirds and butterflies. At the east end of the garden, a miniature forest of dill supported the striped caterpillars that would eventually become swallowtail butterflies, while the wildflower garden on the other side of our driveway was well-loved by all manner of insects, including the bumblebee that one summer day flew inside my shirt, leaving welts on my body the size of dimes. We never referred to these planting beds as pollinator gardens. But that's what they were.

The rest of the property, which most recently had been planted in wheat, my parents seeded back to grasses, cool-season brome for a southern pasture and warm-season native grasses to the north, allowing for year-round grazing for the family horse. My parents were inconsistent environmentalists—they didn't seem to think twice about the number of miles they drove, and most of our meals were served on paper plates, which we burned in an incinerator with the rest of the trash—but they cared deeply about wildlife and understood that our home could provide shelter for more than our family. The prairie grass, especially, offered crucial habitat for native species, from bobwhite quail to hundreds of beneficial insects. Because no one in my family hunted, over time, our home became an informal wildlife refuge, full of turkeys, pheasants, and white-tailed deer. Every day, I woke up aware that what we did as humans—what we built, what we planted—had ripple effects, and not just harmful ones.

Never was this more evident than on burn days. On twenty-six acres, there's always work to do, and we did most of it ourselves, only occasionally hiring a neighbor for a job we didn't have the equipment to complete ourselves. For my brother and I, summer consisted of mowing, weeding, watering, trimming tree sprouts, and harvesting vegetables from the garden. The one job I genuinely looked forward to doing was burning the native grass. Like many North American landscapes, the tallgrass prairie co-evolved with periodic fire, which clears the leaf litter and produces warmer soils and more vigorous growth. Fire also influences when and where ungulates—cattle and bison among them— graze. Indigenous peoples had been burning parts of Kansas since long before my family settled there, and over time the practice was adopted

by everyone from ranchers to people like my father. On our small patch
of prairie, burns never took more than a few hours. But those few hours
were some of the most exciting of the entire year.

A profound lesson was embedded in burn days. Humans, I realized,
are not inherently destructive, but rather can play an active role in
the creation of regenerative landscapes. We have agency in how we shape
the places we inhabit. The status quo of lawns and highly manicured
landscapes is not preordained. We can leave our lands better, healthier,
and more biodiverse than when we arrived.

This idea—the emergence of a worldview that reinserts humans into the
natural world, that sees our species as part of a greater ecological picture—
represents one of the most radical shifts in environmental thought over
the past fifty years. For much of this country's history, ideas about nature
drew a sharp line between human society and the so-called natural world.
As Purdy explains in his book *After Nature*, neither the yeoman farmer,
who was promised redemption in exchange for cultivating an untamed
wilderness, nor the Sierra Club acolyte, for whom the experience of
wilderness was a form of spiritual transcendence, considered themselves
part of that wilderness. Even our current *ecological imagination*, which
emphasizes the interconnectivity of all things, has largely treated human
activity as separate from—and therefore a threat to—nature.

In *Braiding Sweetgrass: Indigenous Wisdom, Scientific Knowledge,
and the Teachings of Plants*, the Potawatomi writer and biologist Robin
Wall Kimmerer tells a story about a graduate student whose thesis
investigated the possible connection between a particular harvesting
technique and an observable decline in sweetgrass (*Hierochloe odorata*) in
the Northeast. Kimmerer had been taught by elders that if humans "use
a plant respectfully, it will stay with [them] and flourish." If they neglect it,
it will disappear. Kimmerer's thesis student planned to measure the impact
of that human use, to put scientific data to the teachings of Kimmerer's
ancestors. In the story, the dean of Kimmerer's college dismissed the idea.
"*Anyone* knows that harvesting a plant will damage the population," the
dean told the student. "You're wasting your time." And yet after two years,

the plots that had been harvested were flourishing, each one "full of new young shoots that signaled a thriving population." It was the control plots, which had not been harvested, that were struggling. "Picking sweetgrass seemed to actually stimulate growth," Kimmerer wrote. "It didn't seem to matter how the grass was harvested, only that it was."

The realities of the Anthropocene disabuse us of the notion that we are separate from nature. We have no choice but to shape the planet. We can do so in ways that plunge the world further into climate chaos, obliterating biodiversity and our own life support systems in the process, or we can do so in ways that enhance the health and well-being of those support systems.

The residential landscapes in this book assert our potential to mold the world in ways that are beneficial and regenerative. Each project takes the climate crisis as its backdrop. The book is organized into four sections or chapters: The first chapter, "Engaging Natural Systems," demonstrates how designers can use local conditions, histories, and ecologies to inform their gardens and site designs. The second chapter, "Restoration and Conservation," focuses on landscapes that actively protect or restore vital and often vulnerable ecosystems. The third chapter, "Building Biodiversity," showcases projects that enhance the local food web, creating conditions for cascading ecological benefits, both on-site and beyond. (The inclusion of Marni Majorelle's Greenwich Avenue rooftop garden in this chapter is a potent reminder that biodiversity goals are compatible even in cities, even on projects no more than thirty-five hundred square feet in size.) The fourth chapter, "Environmental Stewardship," demonstrates the power of landscape to cultivate an ethos of care and restraint, while also publicly questioning systems, attitudes, and preferences that perpetuate harmful garden practices.

The landscapes and gardens collected here traverse region, climate zone, and culture, with examples from across the United States and United Kingdom. The book focuses not on how a particular style or regional aesthetic could be adapted for the changing climate. Instead, it articulates a series of principles that can be applied to most any site or context. These principles are not mutually exclusive, of course, and many of the gardens embrace aspects of each. In the case of Coccoloba Garden in the

Florida Keys, for instance, Raymond Jungles restores native plant communities to both support biodiversity and tie the gardens into a naturally resilient coastal ecosystem.

The principles that form the structure of this book represent an important evolution in residential landscape design. Over the past two decades, as ecological design has become more mainstream, terms like "sustainability" and "resilience" have become diluted—stretched beyond their original definitions to mean almost anything. Resilience has been co-opted by all manner of disciplines, from psychology to finance. We speak of resilient futures, resilient children, resilient housing markets. Sustainability, meanwhile, has become linked to the neoliberal green movement of the early aughts, a catch-all phrase that is, in the words of artist and architectural historian Esther Choi, "interested, by definition, in maintaining the status quo" and is therefore incapable of the transformative work that is necessary to address the climate crisis.

As the effects of our crisis grow more visceral, immediate, and specific, so must our language, for language shapes imagination. Sustainability, if it was ever useful at all, was suited to a world in which climate change was some future threat, a world that had ample time to redirect its energies. The increasing frequency and severity of weather events over the past several years, combined with a growing awareness of their uneven impacts, has made it painfully clear that the climate crisis is here. *Beyond the Garden* assembles examples of domestic landscapes that move beyond vague notions of "sustainability" to achieve something richer and more concrete. Indeed, the title itself is an acknowledgment that what we do in our gardens and the places we call home—that is, if we are fortunate enough to have such a place—has ripple effects far beyond our property lines.

It's worth noting that this book is not a guide or how-to manual for ecological design. Rather, it is meant as inspiration, providing an intimate glimpse into the creativity of some of today's most artful and innovative landscape designers—a portrait of their individual processes. Though future gardeners can learn from what works well in these groundbreaking projects, the mistakes, false assumptions, and happy accidents that the designers humbly share are equally informative. Their stories are a reminder that landscapes are dynamic, and that gardening is as much about watching and noticing as it is about weeding.

If humans and human systems shape the landscape, those landscapes shape us in return. I am writing this introduction during the summer of 2021, more than a year into a global pandemic that has reoriented our relationship to home and place. Home gardening has exploded, overwhelming seed companies and driving a demand for more outdoor space. We are more aware of home and all that it provides us—shelter, comfort, autonomy—than perhaps at any other time in recent history.

At the same time, it is easy (and wise, I think) to be skeptical of the impact of private gardens. A sensitively designed domestic landscape may point the way toward a mended planet, but it can go only so far in reducing global carbon emissions. To address the full scale of the climate crisis, we urgently need political leaders to take bolder action. But if we are to shape the land, if we are to write a human story upon it, the substance of that story matters.

For many of us, our first and perhaps most profound encounter with the natural world happens not while hiking in a national park or kayaking some remote river, but in our own backyards. What we find there informs how we see the world. Reflecting on his own family farm in Hampshire, England, the legendary landscape designer Kim Wilkie puts it this way: "The idea that ecology and responsibility to the natural world is simply about scientific systems…is missing the point. It's about how we relate to the land." This book is an exploration of that relationship through the lens of the places we make. It offers a glimpse of an alternative future—one that all of us must coauthor together.

Engaging
Natural Systems

Amplifying the Ecotone

INTEGRATING SITE SYSTEMS

Project: Whidbey Island Residence
Location: Whidbey Island, Washington
Size: 80 acres
Designer: Berger Partnership

The property on Whidbey Island's southwest corner is hard to find. Just thirty-five miles and a short ferry ride north of Seattle, a network of local roads wind through coniferous forests, cultivated fields, and kettle wetlands. The road fractures into smaller and smaller dirt roads, delving into a dense tapestry of Douglas fir and ponderosa pine. Finally, a two-track gravel driveway rises to a clearing. The native woodland dissolves and a rolling meadow unfolds to the edge of a high bluff—an abrupt horizon revealing the Olympic Mountains across the Puget Sound.

It was, by any measure, a fantastic site, recalls Berger Partnership's Jonathan Morley. When he first arrived there, he remembers thinking, if you did nothing to it, it would still be wonderful. So the question became, "How do you have these [design] interventions but have them not destroy the very thing that you're attracted to in the first place?"

PREVIOUS + BELOW: **Sited between forest and meadow, the house is set back several hundred yards from a high bluff to avoid obstructing scenic views of the island from the Puget Sound.** OVERLEAF: **The only intervention near the bluff is a boulder used for seating.**

Setting the Pace

The clients, a wildlife photographer and a blacksmith, found the property via local word of mouth. For thirty years, they had lived in perfect contentment in a log cabin. Now they wanted to build a new home for their retirement, one that celebrated the remarkable landscape in a way that reflected their values of environmental stewardship.

They made two decisions that set the tone for the rest of the design. First, they placed all but one acre of the eighty-acre property into a permanent conservation easement, limiting their footprint to protect the integrity of the woodland ecology. Second, they envisioned the main residence, guesthouse, and workshop to be set back, several hundred yards away from the waterfront to ensure the buildings' presence didn't mar the scenic character of the coast. They told the design team that when they wanted to enjoy the view from the bluff, they would happily walk there.

OPPOSITE: Green roofs, each planted with native grasses, visually anchor the house to the site. LEFT: When it rains, the roof acts as a sponge, absorbing the runoff and diverting the rest through scuppers to the rain gardens below. BELOW: Water from the roof and gardens is captured and stored in an 8,000-gallon, below-grade cistern. The water is pumped into a filtration system and used to irrigate the landscape and supply household utilities, like toilets and laundry.

Designing within the Ecotone

The primary objective was for the design team to determine the location for the house. This was the third defining decision that set the stage for the integration of the design into its environment. Except for a remnant orchard and prefab pergola—traces of the abandoned homestead—the site was undeveloped when the clients arrived. The architects designed the house to consist of three metal-clad volumes, dubbed the "erratics" in reference to a glacial erratic, a distinctive rock deposited through glacial movement. They placed the house within the ecotone of the forest and meadow, where one rich plant community meets another. The natural gradient experienced in the procession through landscape is acute where the house bridges these two ecologies—a portal from one experience in the landscape to another.

BELOW: A fern grotto is strategically located outside of a central window. The gardens are planted with both native and climate-adapted species, responding to the varying microclimates within the ecotone of the forest and meadow. OPPOSITE: A pillar supporting the covered walkway hovers delicately above a boulder. The entrance opens with dramatic views to the meadow and bluff beyond.

A Procession through the Landscape

On the eastern side of the property, the house is tucked into the forest, emerging from a lush, moist palette of ferns and water-loving grasses. Three verdant roofs of native grasses and wildflowers blanket the erratics, as if pushing them back into the earth.

A parking area for guests is offset from the house by a hundred yards. A gravel path weaves through the native understory, connecting the parking area to a covered walkway that frames the front entrance and opens to massive windows and views of the meadow and bluff beyond. A simple concrete terrace and stone fireplace complete the sequence on the western side of the house. The meadow that borders the bluff was restored to look as uncomplicated and dynamic as it appeared the first time the owners arrived.

Integrated Site Design

The context-sensitive design is a result of the combined expertise of Morley's team with the clients' strong sense of stewardship. The immersive experience conveyed through the integration of the landscape and the architecture at Whidbey is an example of the power of collaborative site design, where the landscape architect, architect, Miller Hull Partnership, and contractors were engaged at the earliest planning stages to effectively connect living and built systems.

"When that integration is thoughtful and your disciplines are collaborating, you can really do some amazing things," Morley said.

LEFT: A concrete terrace lined with gravel meets the meadow.
ABOVE: Windows offer views of the bluff.

LEFT: A concrete terrace extends from the master bedroom. OVERLEAF: The design team carefully regraded the topography to envelope the cedar-clad guest cabin in the forest.

A Symbiotic System

CHANNELING STORMWATER IN THE HIGH DESERT

Project: Woven Plains
Location: Santa Fe, New Mexico
Size: 2.5 acres
Designer: Surroundings Studio

Vibrant layers of native and climate-adapted perennials and ornamental grasses create
an amplified visual experience that transitions into the native landscape.

J ust outside of Santa Fe, northwest of the city, an expanse of
woodland scrub, peppered with piñons and junipers, gradually
rises from the Española basin to the foothills of the Sangre de Cristo
Mountains. A smattering of low-slung, adobe-style houses pop up from
an otherwise seamless expanse of land. The site is situated on a flat, rural-
suburban lot with 270-degree views of the Southern Rocky Mountains
and boundless sky.

When Kenneth Francis of Surroundings Studio was brought in to
the project, the clients had recently relocated to the high desert from the
suburbs of Midland, Texas. Based on years of experience designing in
a desert climate, he established a water ethic from the start of the project.
Francis asked his clients how they wanted to live outside and use their
garden. "This is Santa Fe," Francis reminded them, noting the region's
distinctive ecology, "and I hope that you come here and celebrate it."

The design adapts a centuries-old agricultural technique, known as an acequia, as a piece of modern stormwater infrastructure— a symbiotic irrigation system to support the clients' desire for a lush, vibrant garden in a semiarid landscape.

Site Analysis

The design grew from two strains of analysis—views/privacy and water. Light and sound from the gravel road traveled unobstructed across the level development into the most intimate spaces in the house, including the shower and the bedroom. The clients desired privacy from their few yet highly visible neighbors, but they also wanted to avoid putting up a fence to keep the landscape connected to the surroundings.

Francis's team took what he calls a "perforated approach" to screening. They designed a triangular berm covered in meadow grasses and wildflowers to attenuate sound and car headlights from the road. Weathered steel plates, "dashes in the landscape," selectively mask

The acequia channels stormwater across the site to the leafy "oasis garden" on the opposite side of the property. Water from both the roof of the garage and driveway is diverted into a trench, which is filled with cobble rock and fortified with a pond liner, to efficiently transport the water to a grove of aspens.

views and serve as monolithic backdrops for sculpture and a grove of aspens in what the design team referred to as the "oasis garden," located outside the master bedroom. The clients loved quaking aspens (*Populus tremuloides*)—the sound of delicate leaves fluttering in the wind and the stark juxtaposition of the white bark against the golden fall foliage. Aspens, though common in New Mexico's cooler, higher elevations, prefer consistently moist soil conditions. For the aspens to thrive in the lower, drier plains approaching the city, the design needed to supply the grove with irrigation.

Capturing Runoff

The site analysis revealed that a total of twenty thousand gallons of stormwater per year could be captured from the roofs of the main house and guest casita. The driveway often flooded due to poor drainage, contributing an additional 6,700 usable gallons. Most of the water that fell on the roof of the main house was concentrated over the garage, flowing from the south to southeast—the opposite side of the property from the master bedroom and the aspen grove.

BELOW: The existing landscape before the design. The construction process removed much of the native piñon-juniper woodland scrub around the house. The Surroundings team developed a master plan for the property, creating spaces for social gatherings and relaxation and connecting them to the larger landscape. OVERLEAF: The grove of quaking aspens (*Populus tremuloides*) is drip-irrigated and supplemented with stormwater collected from roofs and other surfaces throughout the site. To keep the soil moist, water is piped into a wick filled with highly porous scoria rock that slowly releases it to the roots of the aspens. Cobble rock covers this subsurface water retention system, which the designer refers to as a water bank.

To capture the water falling on the roof, Francis designed a freestanding, Y-shaped steel trough that channels water from the roof through two canales, or drainage scuppers, into an aboveground cistern. Water stored in the cistern serves raised vegetable beds that the client, an avid cook, can monitor from her kitchen window. Overflow from the cistern is diverted into an acequia, a centuries-old system used for crop irrigation.

The Acequia

The acequia is the spine of the design. Acequias were established in the region by the Pueblo people and expanded by Spanish missionaries. The community-operated system works by diverting water from a major source, such as a river, into a gravity-fed channel that supplies water to smaller trenches that feed agricultural fields. Water not used for irrigation is returned to the source. The term *acequias* was introduced by the Spanish, although Pueblo people did utilize ditches to move water.

BELOW: Stormwater collected from the roof of the main house spills from two canales onto the permeable brick terrace surface. Brick under the roof scuppers is gapped over two drain inlets that pipe the water under the terrace to the aspens' root zones in the oasis garden. Two shades of reclaimed brick define desire lines across the terrace. OPPOSITE TOP: A freestanding steel armature funnels stormwater from the roof into a 650-gallon cistern that stores water for the vegetable garden and landscape irrigation. OPPOSITE BOTTOM: Weathered steel plates screen neighboring properties while framing vistas of the meadows and mountains. OVERLEAF: A triangular plate of steel holds back the grade of a four-foot berm that buffers light and noise from the adjacent gravel road.

The gently sloping watercourse stretches across the property through an eighty-foot trench, cutting across the eastern portion of the site and carrying surface runoff from the driveway and the entertainment terrace to the oasis garden, nourishing the aspen grove.

The acequia's channel articulates a perimeter for the garden without interrupting a connection with the broader landscape. It operates as both a utility, expressing the conveyance of stormwater as a dynamic, integral natural process, and a reflection of the values embedded in the design. It creates a story and an opening for deeper engagement, Francis explained: "It threads a message around a landscape that benefits from this system."

OPPOSITE TOP LEFT: Though Santa Fe receives an average of thirteen inches of rain per year, its semiarid climate causes surface water to evaporate and infiltrate quickly into the sandy soil, making water conservation crucial. OPPOSITE TOP RIGHT: The planting is mostly native with low-water-demand species that thrive in Santa Fe's climate. The meadow was seeded with native grasses and wildflowers—such as Mexican hat plant (*Ratibida columnifera*)—providing habitat value in the more open portions of the landscape. OPPOSITE BOTTOM: Catmint (*Nepeta x faassenii*), sheep fescue (*Festuca ovina*), and Helen von Stein lambs ear (*Stachys byzantina* 'Helen von Stein') with pockets of blue avena grass (*Helictotrichon sempervirens*), line the perimeter of the eastern terrace, a space designed for stargazing and smoking cigars. Maiden hair grass (*Miscanthus sinensis* 'Gracillimus') provides a green backdrop to the seating.

Tracing Terrain

ENGAGING SURFACE CHARACTER FOR GROUNDWATER RECHARGE

Project: Farrar Pond Residence
Location: Lincoln, Massachusetts
Size: 3 acres
Designer: Mikyoung Kim Design

Snow exaggerates the contours of the kettle and kame topography, a remnant of glacial deposits along New England's coastal plains.

It was January when landscape architect Mikyoung Kim first visited the property southwest of Lincoln. A huge snowstorm made it impossible to navigate the driveway, and the boots she was wearing weren't tall enough for the deluge of snow blanketing the land. Kim returned to the site throughout the seasons, yet it was her first encounter, after a storm, that stuck with her, setting in motion a language for the design: "Snow has this capacity to simplify the undulations of the landscape."

Farrar Pond

The three-acre property is tucked into the native hardwood forests surrounding Farrar Pond, a stone's throw from iconic Walden Pond and one of hundreds of ponds, both naturally occurring and constructed, stretching across New England's inland coastal plains. Farrar was originally a low-lying, wet meadow. It was flooded in early 1900 by Ed Farrar, a man who owned a portion of the property and who wanted to retain it as a permanent body of water by his home. Well before it was a meadow, glaciers shaped the kettle holes and kame terraces that roll beneath the region's woodlands, fields, and bodies of water. The design is intimately linked to this terrain, expressing an intrinsic connection between the surface within the garden and the broader landscape.

Capturing Runoff

The clients wanted something artful, unexpected, and, of course, functional. A space for entertainment and relaxation, for their grandkids to play and two German shepherds to roam. Conscious of their landscape's impact on the surrounding environment, they did not want an irrigation system, chemical maintenance, or a lawn. Kim took their wishes one step further by removing all the asphalt on the property and replacing it with porous surfaces, like granular materials and bluestone paving, so the rainwater could percolate into the soil, recharging the groundwater table.

In lieu of lawn, Kim's design employed low-growing ground cover (referred to as "stepables"), such as sedum and a mix of thyme, to ensure that the stormwater falling on the site goes through an ecological cleansing process before entering Farrar Pond. The ground cover is planted between strips of bluestone pavers scattered through a series of garden "rooms," representative of species in the surrounding forest: the evergreen room (consisting of eastern white pine), the river birch room, and the paper birch room, each expressing distinct responses to the changing seasons.

Watching the landscape emerge over time is "like meeting a new person," Kim said. "Finding out who they are, what they want to be and how they're going to actually transform as they age through the seasons."

ABOVE: Farrar Pond from the surrounding woodlands. LEFT: The Corten steel fence traces the perimeter of the site, providing protected space for the clients' dogs to roam. OPPOSITE: The landscape architects conducted an analysis of the site to determine where water was flowing and where it needed to be retained to percolate into the earth. Bluestone pavers run throughout the landscape.

Beyond the fence, perennial grasses are interspersed with the understory of the native hardwood forest at the edges of the property. "Everything was woven together, not on an object-by-object basis, but as a tapestry," designer Mikyoung Kim said.

Migrating Form

A fence traces a portion of the property, stringing together the garden rooms with a contiguous, migrating weathered form. The site appears flat, but it was carefully regraded to reference the nuanced rise and fall of the postglacial terrain. As the fence travels across the landscape, it articulates the subtle undulations of the surface, acting as both a piece of sculpture and as a functional barrier to contain the clients' dogs on the property.

Beyond the fence, a path weaves through the forest and down to the water. On one visit, Kim came across a grove of birch trees that had fallen haphazardly, crisscrossing the path—unmanicured, evolving. It's possible that this is where the inspiration for the paving came from, though it's hard to pinpoint exactly. The client recently told her: "It looks like the voids from the fence actually fell out and became the paving pattern." "I thought that was very poetic," Kim said.

At its widest, the fence is the shoulder-to-shoulder dimension of the clients' dogs, just narrow enough so they can't escape. Similarly, the pavers provide protection and structure for the plants that grow around the fence and allow for an evolving green tapestry. "Landscapes don't exist in a fixed state of green," observed Kim.

The existing asphalt driveway was replaced with permeable pavers and continues the interwoven pattern to the base of the house. The design for the ground plane focuses on durability. The pavers, for example, help bear the weight of much of the foot traffic protecting the ground cover.

OPPOSITE: "Gardens are one of the most important places we make as landscape architects," Kim explained. "They are the place where we all learn about our place in the world and how the daily impacts we make can transform the environment that we live in." TOP: The location of the fence was determined on-site as the design team walked the perimeter of the garden. BOTTOM: The fence was fabricated off-site; each Corten steel bar is screwed together with a peg at a joint connecting the individual pieces. The pieces were folded and transported in seven modular units.

Recovering Site Character

RECYCLING STONE IN SANTA BARBARA

Project: Pedregosa
Location: Santa Barbara, California
Size: 4,800 square feet
Designer: Grace Design Associates

The house on Pedregosa Street was vacant before Margie Grace and her design team started digging. The excavation in preparation for the new home and landscape revealed leftover curb stone and smaller pieces of rubble buried beneath the weeds and overgrown shrubs. They would use it, Grace thought, she just didn't know how. They put the material aside and kept digging.

Next, they found boulders, piled over a century ago into a channel to fill an ephemeral creek that runs through the neighborhood. Some of the rock had been worked, sculpted by stone masons in the past, reflecting periods of craftsmanship dating back to the 1870s when the one-third-acre property was a small piece of a larger estate stretching across the entire block. They sorted the rocks according to size and continued to dig, uncovering over two hundred cubic yards of sandstone buried under the historic city lot.

The sandstone excavated from the site was recycled back into the landscape to create mounds, walls, and steps. OVERLEAF: Grasses and boulders connect the main house and artist studio. Anything and everything from the excavation that could be repurposed was conserved and layered back into the design—an important step in reducing the environmental impact of material production and transportation.

Recycling History

The clients were originally from Iowa. An internationally renowned artist and a Broadway singer, they approached Grace with a vision for a contemplative yet lively space, evocative of their Midwestern roots but also appropriate to Santa Barbara's Mediterranean climate, one that required minimal maintenance and aligned with their creative approach to life and commitment to sustainability.

Together, Grace and the clients decided to salvage all the rock uncovered during the excavation and recycle it back into the design of the landscape. The design process was highly collaborative, Grace said, guided by the clients' artistic expression and deeply rooted in the historic character of the site. The design was about "painting the picture with the fewest brush strokes," she said.

Sandstone boulders with flat faces were used as steps, terracing down from a cedar hot tub to amphitheater-style seating around a firepit and a gravel stage.

A Story of Stonework

Sandstone is a distinguishing feature of Santa Barbara's landscape. Readily found in local creek beds and canyons, it was a staple building material for the earliest settlers, including the Chumash and later the Spanish missionaries. Pedregosa, meaning "rocky" in Spanish, is the name of the street that bisects El Pueblo Viejo, the city's historic district. Wander around the neighborhood, and "you can see everything from stacked up field stone to heavily worked, refined stonework," explained Grace.

On the clients' property, Grace used excavated curb stone and rubble to build walls and terraces, allowing the natural character of the found material to dictate the style of construction and convey a narrative of local human occupation through history. In the front of the house along the street, she restored an existing cut-stone wall, built during a period of Italian craftsmanship and set with mortar. Perpendicular to the historic wall, Grace built a looser, dry-stacked wall, each piece carefully fit together and held in place by gravity. At first, the clients thought the wall appeared too refined, too meticulously placed by the human hand, so they drove into it with a tractor, allowing pieces to fall and form a more organic, weathered edge. The new wall, juxtaposed with the clean lines of the Italian masonry, represents "something of a relic left from before," Grace said.

BELOW LEFT: Large stone pavers and Mexican beach pebbles create a generous procession to the front entrance of the main house. BELOW RIGHT: The stone from the front walkway that would not split was used to create steps behind the house.

Larger boulders from the excavation and imported soil were used to make mounds, adding dimension and definition to the previously flat landscape and rerouting an existing stream to drain away from the house. Grace placed the smaller boulders, interspersed with tufts of succulents and ornamental grasses, to poke out of the mounds, as if they were outcroppings, emerging as they would in an alluvial plain as the soil erodes away into the water.

TOP LEFT AND RIGHT: Before the existing home was demolished, it was used as a canvas for local graffiti artists. The installation was up for less than a week before the demolition. Materials were salvaged and donated for reuse as building materials. BOTTOM: The original site was flat, with compacted soil in need of reshaping for proper drainage. Designer Margie Grace used the excavated stone to add dimension to the landscape by creating large, boulder-studded mounds using excess soil from a nearby site. The house, which sits low on the property, was subject to flooding from what was once an ephemeral stream that had been piped directly under the master bedroom. Grace used the mounds to create a "moat" that redirected the stream to circumvent the house and flow into swales planted with water-efficient grasses.

The New House on the Block

Unlike the ubiquitous presence of sandstone walls throughout the city, the architectural character of the homes in the El Pueblo Viejo neighborhood is varied. Historic, adobe structures dating back to the early twentieth century are mixed in with Tudors, mid-century-modern houses, and craftsman-style bungalows. The clients' house is a prefabricated model called the Sunset Breezehouse by architect Michelle Kaufmann and one of a few contemporary structures on the block. Before the old house was demolished, the clients invited local artists to use it as a canvas, covering it in graffiti and sculpture.

The installation caused a stir. "It split the neighborhood," Grace said. "I mean there were letters to the editor about [the art] inviting gangs." Seventy-two hours later, independent of the uproar, it was gone, loaded into a truck and hauled off to make way for the new house. The style of new house sparked similar tumult. Everyone had an opinion about it, according to Grace, and she celebrates that difference. "You get twenty piles of rocks and twenty people and say, 'stack these up into a wall.' Amazingly, you have walls that look really different."

A dry-stacked stone wall—a loose construction made with stone excavated from the site—runs perpendicular to the more formal mortar-set wall that lines the street. Grasses balance the weight of the stone, adding lightness and texture to the landscape. The design uses Mexican feathergrass (*Nassella tenuissima*), a once-popular, drought-tolerant ornamental grass that is no longer recommended for planting in California landscapes, particularly near wildland areas, Grace noted, as it reseeds itself and overtakes native species.

Composing the Urban Landscape

In the 1870s, long before the neighborhood had been divided into smaller lots as it is today, the owner of the estate built a water tower, which still stands as a historic landmark. The clients' lot is directly adjacent to the neighbor whose property now includes the tower, which is a noticeable presence in the clients' garden, its ornate style unmissable amid the tree canopy.

Grace incorporated it visually into the home's new landscape, framing it at the end of a path between tufts of grasses, boulders, and a large Victorian box (*Pittosporum undulatum*) with the neighbor's pines beyond. The path leads from the Italian stone wall at the edge of the property, winding loosely through the garden to a firepit set in gravel and surrounded by amphitheater-style seating. The clients often gathered there for impromptu performances. As it happens, the neighbor with the tower is also a musician, a concert pianist. They installed a gate between their properties, and together they enjoy duets and sunset cocktails in the tower.

OPPOSITE: Grace embraced the juxtaposition of the modern garden with the historic water tower, integrating it into the garden composition through layers of planting.

Wildness, in Context

THE ANTI-GARDEN AND THE PARADOX OF REWILDING

Project: The Anti-Garden
Location: Sussex, England
Size: 4 acres
Designer: Jinny Blom

A pond planted with various aquatic species sits below
a low, stacked stone wall. Blom first tested the concept of
an anti-garden at a project in the Scottish Highlands, where
she restored indigenous species into the landscape, all the
while making the architecture of the house disappear.

The garden at Sussex Farm is a "natural isotope," Jinny Blom explained, "where you draw in as much life as you possibly can into the place that you're making in the hope that it will then seed out into the wider landscape." Blom calls it an "anti-garden"; it is nature, augmented.

The anti-garden dissolves the rules of a traditional garden. It is ephemeral and abundant, evoking a sense of endless discovery. Though it appears "wild," with life emerging from every crack in the stone walkways, the anti-garden is neither unmanaged nor passive. It is highly contextualized and intentional—free in spirit yet rooted firmly in place.

The Scottish Highlands and Sussex Farm

The concept for the Anti-Garden in Sussex began on a different project for the same client some five hundred miles north in the Scottish Highlands, where Blom wanted to make the house disappear into the rugged terrain and to restore a landscape that had been degraded from years of use for hunting and commercial forestry.

"You have to have a deep understanding of the land before you can start to subvert it," Blom said. When she arrived, the landscape was wild but not native. There was little wildlife, and the once thriving aquatic and plant ecosystems had been depleted. It was overgrazed and overpopulated with Sitka spruce, imported from Maine during the Scottish Victorian era. "I had a 65,000-acre weed issue with the spruce as they seed freely and dominate indigenous species," Blom said. Creating a wild garden, she added, "is not romantic nonsense. It's highly researched."

She installed eleven miles of fencing to keep the deer out. Within a year, without the pressures from grazing and with the introduction of a native seed bank, the landscape regenerated with astonishing speed, transforming what was once a seemingly barren area into a rambling garden teeming with life.

OPPOSITE: **To ground the garden in the local landscape, Blom used plants that appear to be wild—cultivars of plants like columbine (*Aquilegia*), fennel (*Foeniculum vulgare*), and great burnet (*Sanguisorba officinalis*), which grow naturally in the surrounding area.** ABOVE: **At Sussex Farm, Blom aimed to subvert the traditional conception of a garden, allowing the design to absorb the home back into the landscape, in turn pulling to the foreground an intrinsic sense of history and place.**

After completing the garden in the Scottish Highlands, the client asked Blom to create another one on their property in Sussex on England's southeastern flank. When she first arrived at the site, a former dairy farm, the landscape was "suspiciously green," Blom recalled, with three birch trees stranded in a few acres of carefully striped lawn. The client wanted to create a garden that was imbued with a sense of infinite freedom. "It needed to be an anti-garden because you don't want it to feel legislated, and gardens are legislated things," Blom said.

The Edible Garden

The property is located in a region of iron foundries that used ironstone, a sedimentary rock derived from thick beds of boulder clay over stone. The garden itself is surrounded by woodlands, which includes species like sweet chestnut, oak, lime, hazel, and ash that were once coppiced frequently to regenerate timber, in part to fuel the foundry operations.

BELOW: **Flowering perennials and grasses are planted right at the edge of the pool, immersing it in the garden.** OPPOSITE: **A fragrant, rambling rose (*Rosa filipes*) blooms as lichen grows on weathered stone.**

Of the property's four hundred acres, Blom used four to create an entirely productive landscape with edible, medicinal, and other multifunctional plants. She planted nutteries, orchards, coppices, and meadows, as well as a vegetable garden in the front of the house. In lieu of a fence to keep out deer, Blom planted a thicket of hawthorn bushes with a variety of native shrubs to create a species-rich hedgerow around the perimeter. Within the garden, fences built from cleft chestnut are woven with raspberries, blackberries, and loganberries. What people don't eat, the birds consume, Blom noted.

The garden is organized into a series of intersecting rooms, following the orthogonal design logic of a traditional English garden. The seemingly overgrown, untamed plantings create a dreamy sense of anticipation and discovery, while the overall structure of the design enforces an intuitive network for circulation. To blend the garden into the broader landscape, Blom used cultivars of species that have a close relationship to wild plants in appearance. In the cutting garden, for example, she used cultivars of plants like columbine (*Aquilegia*), fennel (*Foeniculum vulgare*), and great burnet (*Sanguisorba officinalis*), all of which grow in the surrounding area.

BELOW: **A path mowed through a meadow of native grasses and wildflowers reaches a line of espaliered trees anchored by mounding shrubs at their bases.**

The Paradox of Rewilding the Garden

There is an illusion that a wild landscape, seemingly untended by the human hand, involves no planning or maintenance; that allowing plants to grow and spread, intermingling naturally, will automatically create the soft, patinated quality of a well-aged garden. Wildness needs to be contextualized, and, as Blom discovered when she designed the first anti-garden in Scotland, translating wilderness onto the domestic garden requires research and a deep understanding of the history of a place.

"It's hubristic to say, 'I am rewilding my land,'" Blom said. "You don't rewild land, land rewilds itself if we disappear." That's the anti-garden: "It's a garden that is all about nature and all about our tinkering with it," Blom said. "Because anything you tinker with is a garden in the end."

Restoration
and Conservation

Restoring Lost Ecologies

HISTORIC PRESERVATION IN COASTAL ACADIA

Project: Northeast Harbor
Location: Mount Desert Island, Maine
Size: 5 acres
Designer: STIMSON

The woodlands of Acadia stretch from the mainland to Mount Desert Island along the rocky headlands of coastal Maine. Charles William Eliot, the former president of Harvard University and a pioneer of the landscape preservation movement in the United States, built a summer home at the base of the mountains along the rugged coast in 1879. For nearly forty years, Eliot worked in collaboration with philanthropist John D. Rockefeller Jr. and ardent conservationist George B. Dorr, known as the Father of Acadia, to protect the scenic area until it was declared the first national park on the East Coast in 1916.

"It has this incredible legacy of being completely connected to the roots of landscape preservation in our country and even the world," designer Lauren Stimson said, suggesting that the master planning for Acadia National Park may have happened on this property. Perhaps even more significant, Eliot's son, the younger Charles Eliot, a landscape architect and regional planner, would go on to found the Trustees of Reservations, the country's first conservation organization of its kind. Undoubtedly, his time on Mount Desert Island and exposure to the origins of Acadia laid the groundwork for his influential career in conservation and land preservation.

Unfortunately, when Stimson and her team arrived at the site, a five-acre slice of Eliot's former 120-acre property, the history embedded in the local ecology had been all but erased. The land had been blasted in preparation for the construction of the new home, leaving a massive hole where a few remaining conifers clung to a thin layer of topsoil sitting on nearly a foot of ledge.

PREVIOUS: Prior to developing the design for this project, Stimson took note of the species diversity in the regional ecologies of Acadia. Jordan Pond, for example, a 187-acre lake carved into the mountainous terrain by glaciers, proximate to the site, has its own microclimate, a swamp ecosystem, marsh grasses, and a different type of shrub layer than the surrounding ecology. BELOW: A stream runs from the mountains of Acadia National Park through the property. Stimson restored the riparian zone with moss, wetland grasses, and woody shrubs to stabilize the banks. OPPOSITE: The design pays homage the site's rich ecological and cultural history, connecting the property back to the local native landscape through careful restoration efforts informed by extensive research.

Restoration

Stimson delved into historic photos and literature about the area.
Since Eliot's time, she discovered, the local landscape had lost species
diversity and transitioned from an open, summit meadow ecology to
a primarily climax forest dominated by spruce. The restoration efforts
were extensive, unfolding over several years, to mitigate the damage
from the blasting and restore the native planting to reflect the ecology
characteristic of the area when Acadia first became a national park.

The shallow soil profile was a critical issue. As the designers
developed plans for the landscape, occasional winter storms with winds
exceeding seventy miles per hour swept across the coast. "All of these
climax spruce trees would basically blow over like candlesticks. It was
so discouraging," Stimson said. "We'd show up on the site, and we would
have lost another handful of trees because they were growing on ledge.
The surface area for soil is so thin. Their root systems were intertwined
and became a mat that would flip over."

Stimson and her team worked with a soil-science firm, Pine and Swallow Environmental, to build up soil to provide a stable foundation for new planting and remove remnant pieces of talus that had accumulated after the blasting from the previous construction. They used organic soil amendments, sourced locally, like lobster and crab shell from Southwest Harbor, well-aged leaf compost from the landfill, and local granitic sand from Lamoine, Maine. They brought in hundreds of trees—including mature spruce to screen views from the neighbors; a younger, mixed-spruce nurse crop; balsam fir and birch; an understory of shadbush, winterberry, and bunchberry; and a deciduous layer of witch hazel and red maple.

OPPOSITE + RIGHT:
Steel plates echo the strains of gabbro, an igneous rock, seen in outcroppings throughout the site.

Curated Wild

After the ecological restoration efforts, Stimson's intervention was intentionally restrained. The design celebrated the native landscape through a series of understated overlooks, strategically placed along a path, leading from the main house down to the water. She laid out granite steps with spans of gravel to traverse the steep, coastal terrain. As the path retreats from the main house, the character of the materials and planting loosens, dissolving back into the native landscape that originally inspired Stimson's preservation efforts.

The clients are renowned art collectors. Accordingly, the landscape adjacent to the house is distinctly curated. Linear bands of low-bush blueberry and hay-scented fern are organized into patterns that relate to the fenestration of the building and create a border for the kids' play lawn and swing set. For the woodland paving, Stimson used local reclaimed rustic granite from an abandoned quarry, and around the dwellings, a Woodbury gray granite from Vermont with both thermal and split face intrusions, a combination meant to ground the distinctly modern architecture.

BELOW: An overlook is nestled just off one of the paths to the water, an unassuming gesture that provides no more than a flat plane to view the landscape. OPPOSITE: The design loosens as it extends through the woodlands and to the water, while the areas nearest to the house provide functional spaces for the homeowners and their young children.

The Path

Two footpaths split just outside of the main house at the edge of the woods. As they wind through the canopy, the paths meet a series of Corten steel plates embedded into the earth to create level planes for quiet terraces overlooking the water. The plates are conceived of as "strokes," or dashes, across the landscape. "One stroke is holding up the main house, another is defining the ledge, and the last one is holding up the guest house," Stimson said, adding that the steel plates reference the grains of native gabbro striations seen in the exposed ledge outcropping.

Just below the ledge slope, two stone footbridges span streams that flow as ribbons down from the Acadia mountains, across the site, and into the Atlantic. Along the stream corridors, Stimson placed boulders, planted with moss, and added wetland grasses and woody shrubs to mitigate erosion along the banks. The stormwater from the main house and landscape above is captured in a swale just north of the guesthouse, where the two paths meet. There, the treatment of the stone becomes more rugged. Chiseled, split-faced granite steps and a crushed stone pathway navigate the forty-foot elevation change between the main house and the guesthouse below.

A granite staircase descends to the final stretch of the path, where the steps continue along a fern-lined walkway that leads down to the water, completing the procession from the woodlands to the coast. The footprint of Eliot's original boathouse sits here, at the base of the site, in the shadow of Acadia National Park and before a pier reaching into the Atlantic. While the design interventions are distinctly modern, the materials palette is regional, and the plant communities remain familiar and indigenous. The result is a thriving and diverse landscape created on a previously devastated site, in honor of Eliot's primitive piece of coastal Maine.

Tending the Native Garden
BENEFICIAL DISTURBANCES IN ECOLOGICAL GARDENING

Project: Millersville Meadows and Garden
Location: Millersville, Pennsylvania
Size: 2.8 acres
Designer: Larry Weaner Associates

"Interestingly, a lot of the things you learn to do in horticulture are counterproductive in the world of ecology, particularly in maintaining it," Larry Weaner said. His work reimagines the potential of the residential garden as an opportunity to support local ecologies by restoring native landscapes and teaching people how to care for them.

At the garden in Millersville, a rural enclave west of Philadelphia, the client's old gardening habits proved hard to break and ultimately triggered an unexpected yet enlightening succession of plants in the garden.

Ecological Gardening

The client, a sophisticated horticulturalist, maintained extensive, though not necessarily native, gardens on her previous property. When she and her partner approached Weaner about designing the landscape around their new home, which sits on nearly three acres, she expressed an interest in using only native species and transitioning to a more ecologically focused approach to maintenance.

Weaner designed and installed a native understory of herbaceous perennials and woody plants around the house, including a shaded woodland garden with a water feature. In front of the house, he installed a meadow that sweeps down to the road. For maintaining the gardens, Weaner's advice was to cut the weeds, other than the most pernicious, at the base, not pull them by the roots.

BELOW + PREVIOUS: A mowed path through the native meadow and woodlands beyond.

"Every time you pull a weed, you get twelve," he said, because of the soil disturbance uprooting causes. Plants produce and disperse seeds, and under the appropriate climatic conditions, will germinate and begin developing into a new plant. Disturbances to the soil, like removing a plant by the roots, encourages germination in the soil seed bank, the mostly dormant seeds that are stored in the soil. Like many residential landscapes, the client's seed bank was initially composed of primarily weed seeds.

Against Weaner's advice, the client, being the diligent gardener she is, could not let a weed go unpulled. "She just couldn't shake gardening," Weaner laughed, adding that "even today, she's still pulling up weeds."

The Native Seed Bank

One recent spring, many years after Weaner completed the project, he visited again only to find the garden full of columbine (*Aquilegia*), a native perennial, dotting the landscape with red and yellow flowers. After so many years, columbine should have been long gone, Weaner said, outcompeted by the more aggressive perennial species. Columbine's unanticipated presence was due to a shift in the composition of the landscape's seed bank. Over the last decade, the native plants had been producing and dispersing millions of seeds, slowly dominating the weed seeds. So now, each time the client pulls a weed, encouraging seed germination, the new plant that emerges is more likely to be a native species rather than a weed. Furthermore, the occasional small, scattered disturbances also spurred regeneration within the native species, allowing new perennials to replace older ones and reinvigorating the native plant community.

For Weaner, witnessing the unexpected composition of the garden was illuminating. "Her pulling by the roots, which I was dissuading her from doing in the beginning, is now maybe a healthy disturbance," he said. "Now you're not so worried about weed seeds [in the seed soil bank] because they've diminished over the years; those little weeding disturbances may be an ideal disturbance regime, whereas in the beginning they were just an opening for weeds."

The Neighborhood

Upon seeing the success of the client's garden, the neighbors across the street installed a native meadow in their front yard too. Soon after, the neighbor next door followed suit, and today, meadows sweep across the landscape, providing a dramatic entry to the neighborhood.

OPPOSITE: The yellow bloom of the golden groundsel (*Packera aurea*) sweeps across the property in the summer months.
LEFT: Weaner stabilized and planted the walls of a historic remnant limekiln on the property with native perennials.

OPPOSITE TOP: A flagstone path winds through the native gardens around the house. OPPOSITE BOTTOM: Columbine (*Aquilegia*) and wild blue phlox (*Phlox divaricata*) intermingle with native grasses in the meadow around the house. ABOVE: A tapestry of perennials thrives in the native garden. LEFT: The neighbors' meadows line the entrance to the community.

OVERLEAF: A shaded water feature in the woodland garden.

A Seamless Connection

MEDIATING BOUNDARIES AT THE URBAN-WILDLAND INTERFACE

Project: Ketchum Residence
Location: Ketchum, Idaho
Size: 0.5 acres
Designer: Lutsko Associates

The plant palette forges a visual connection with the broader landscape by blending the grasslands of the foothills with a curated palette of native species adjacent to the house. A simple deer fence is the sole delineation of the property's edge.

By May, months of snow cover in Idaho's Wood River Valley give way to an explosion of seasonal color as the grasslands bloom in the lengthening spring and summer days in the high desert climate. Located just outside the town of Ketchum, this property abuts the rugged foothills of the Sawtooth Mountains and is surrounded by single-family homes. On his first visit to the then-undeveloped property, landscape architect Ron Lutsko recalled how the grasslands from the foothills swept into the empty lot, interrupting the monotonous pattern of lawn- and spruce-covered yards in the suburban enclave with the dynamic yet uncomplicated beauty of the native landscape.

Grounded in Local Ecology

By dissolving the property line into the foothills beyond, Lutsko created the sense that standing on the half-acre lot felt like being on a thousand-acre ranch. The design forges a visual connection with the larger ecosystem by weaving hyperlocal plant species found in the nearby meadows into the immediate landscape around the house. The landscape is designed and experienced as a gradient, compressed near the architecture and loosening as the garden merges into the hillside.

At the perimeter, an array of native grasses and wildflowers blend with the existing grasslands as a form of "orchestrated restoration" to help rebuild areas of the property impacted by the construction of the house. In the approach to the house, the plant palette is refined as the local species are layered with plants selected for seasonal color and hues of silvers against greens. Along the entry staircase, the planting is further simplified, distilled into bands of a singular species contained on subtle terraces extending from the steps. Behind the house, a seating area and a small section of lawn enclosed by low-concrete walls serve as an extension of the interior and a space for gathering with exceptional views of the mountains.

RIGHT: The landscape flourishes without artificial support systems, requiring little maintenance and no irrigation once the plants were established. OPPOSITE TOP: In the approach to the house, the native meadow is distilled into monocultures, planted in bands along terraces extending from the steps. Great Basin wild rye (*Leymus cinereus*), chamisa (*Ericameria nauseosa*), and other species are layered against the concrete pavilion, while firecracker penstemon (*Penstemon eatonii*) bloom in the foreground as the design blends with the native meadow. OPPOSITE BOTTOM: Blue flax (*Linum usitatissimum*) and yarrow (*Achillea*) bloom in the meadow beyond the patio. Reflective glass windows mirror the landscape.

TOP: Perennials catch the light along the concrete and natural steel entry stairs. Blue flax and penstemon mingle with meadow grasses in the foreground. BOTTOM: A simple gravel footpath provides a walkway through the meadow and around the house.

Supporting Habitat with Native Species

The house consists of two concrete pavilions with courtyards woven in between. Enormous panels of reflective-glass windows capture impressions of Great Basin wild rye, goldenrod, geranium, yarrow, and chamisa, mirroring a tapestry of native species back into the landscape. Given the site's proximity to a natural ecosystem, Lutsko used exclusively native plants, highlighting the intrinsic beauty of the landscape while simultaneously rebuilding the habitat of the local ecosystem.

"I believe first and foremost in trying to use a native plant, and that's primarily because it supports local fauna," Lutsko said, adding that appropriate maintenance practices are crucial to ensuring the habitat benefits of a native landscape. Take, for example, the western blue flag (*Iris missouriensis*), a type of wild iris found throughout the western United States, which blooms in late spring and provides a critical habitat for spiders indigenous to the region. When the seed heads die later in the summer, its appearance is often perceived as untidy, but Lutsko offers a caution: "If you cut off that blue flag seed head, what you're doing is also cutting off a spider's egg sack," thus destroying its habitat. Because of the spider's intrinsic value as a food source for other animals and a beneficial predator, eating insects harmful to the local plant population, removing its habitat in the seed head interrupts the balance of the ecosystem and reduces its overall species diversity.

Formalized areas for seating and entertaining are limited in size and treated as an extension of the house. "I'm a believer that people should learn to appreciate the nature they're living with," designer Ron Lutsko said.

The Pipevine Swallowtail

While using native plants was an integral part of the design in Ketchum, in other projects, climate and place-appropriate non-native species can also be beneficial, believes Lutsko, a point he has tested at his own garden on a farm in California, where he experiments with a variety of native and non-native plants. On the farm, where he keeps extensive gardens and tests drought-tolerant and climate-appropriate species, he has found a non-native flowering perennial that supports a local butterfly population, the pipevine swallowtail. The butterfly is so named because, as a caterpillar, it feeds exclusively on the California native pipevine (*Aristolochia californica*), a deciduous vine with distinctive tube-shaped flowers common in northern and central California. Lutsko came to notice that a rare species of echium, a perennial with nectar that attracts pollinators endemic to the Canary Islands, also attracted the pipevine swallowtail. The echium blooms later in the season than native California nectar plants, extending the food supply for butterflies. According to Lutsko, he has tenfold the number of butterflies on his farm because of the echium.

"I am an avid believer in having plants be appropriate to a place," he said, adding that having tough, drought-tolerant plants that don't have to be supported technologically or artificially are ideal, even if they are not 100 percent native.

OPPOSITE TOP: A glazed gate, designed by artist Ned Kahn, filters light as a delicate grid onto a poplar tree in a courtyard. OPPOSITE BOTTOM: The Sawtooth Mountains and the grasslands that cover the foothills bordering the property inspired a landscape design grounded in the intrinsic character of the local ecology.

Oaks and the Arroyo

DESIGNING FOR SCALE AND CONTINUITY
IN THE SAN GABRIEL FOOTHILLS

Project: Arroyo Seco
Location: San Marino, California
Size: 1.4 acres
Designer: Elysian Landscapes

The original plan for this project was to replace the existing house, which was modest in scale but iconic in style at the edge of an approximately one-and-one-half-acre lot outside of Los Angeles, with a single-family residence. It would need to accommodate a fluctuating tide of guests, from intimate family gatherings to social events of one hundred or more.

As the scale of this would-be home grew, the plan was scrapped, and a new vision grew from what was already there. The clients would preserve the historic home nestled into the sloping topography of a foothill woodland landscape studded with magnificent coast live oaks.

Connecting the Dots

Designed by architect Calvin Straub, the house is a classic mid-century-modern structure with ample glass and angular geometry articulating the landscape as an extension of the home. Two smaller structures dotted the property—an old pergola and a garage adjacent to the house. The pergola was transformed into a ceramics workspace, and the garage became a photography studio and library. The clients added three new structures—a pool pavilion, gym, and guesthouse—creating a residential microcampus with the landscape as the unifying element.

The challenge for the garden was twofold: create continuity between the historic and contemporary architecture and the existing landscape and mediate the scale of the campus, keeping in mind the number of guests the clients frequently entertain. The landscape "had to be able to flex," Elysian Landscapes' Judy Kameon noted, "but still feel intimate when it was just a summer dinner or drink by the firepit."

BELOW: **The property before the landscape design. The garage was converted to the photography studio and library.** OPPOSITE: **The burgundy hues of Bloodgood Japanese maple (***Acer palmatum*** 'Bloodgood') are woven into a tapestry of shade-tolerant, low-water shrubs and ground cover, framing the pool pavilion beyond. The planting provides screening from neighbors while articulating functional spaces for social gatherings.**

BELOW: A decomposed granite path winds through the landscape of native oaks and a warm understory palette. Hardscape is limited to areas of daily foot traffic, while a secondary and tertiary network of paths links the built structures scattered throughout the property. OPPOSITE: A low, board-formed concrete retaining wall defines the kitchen garden in front of the photography studio and library. Here, in one of the few full-sun areas of the property, Kameon planted a mix of edibles and ornamental plants for year-round interest, and flowers for cutting and attracting pollinators and wildlife. Rather than a chemically treated lumber, the steps and raised planter bed are made of cedar, which is naturally impervious to insects.

The Oaks and the Arroyo

San Marino's climate is mild and temperate, which supports a wide range of plant species. Kameon expressed the site's climatic character with an abundant palette of native, Mediterranean, and subtropical species, providing a lush counterpoint to the crisp simplicity of the architecture. The planting serves as a bridge between the curated garden and the rich ecology of the Arroyo Seco, an ephemeral riverbed running through the steep canyons of the San Gabriel foothills to the Los Angeles River.

The selection of plants was based on the distinctive growing requirements of the existing oaks that cast intermittent pockets of shade throughout the property. During the construction process, careful consideration was taken to avoid disturbing the soil conditions around the dripline. Kameon avoided planting water-demanding species at their base, as established oaks do best in nonirrigated soils. Extended periods of moisture during the warm summer months can damage the root system and lead to the proliferation of root-disease fungi.

To create a sense of continuity, Kameon said, "I didn't want to have sharp breaks from shade to sun," so the transition had to be seamless. Both native and climate-appropriate, dry-shade species line the perimeter of the canopy, radiating out into a tapestry of green hues, woven together with tones of gold and burgundy in mounding layers of shrubs and ground covers and punctuated with structural succulents and clumps of grasses.

Logic, Scale, Connection

Kameon designed a path network that creates an intuitive hierarchy for circulation. Durable pads of concrete and stone form the primary paths for the everyday foot traffic to the main house and to the key entertainment spaces. The secondary path network is narrower, articulated with cast-in-place concrete pavers with planted joints, connecting the areas for social gathering with the structures around the property. The tertiary layer of decomposed granite footpaths winds through the outer edges of the landscape.

Visible from the front entry and main house is a highly focal green roof that was retrofitted onto the garage-turned-photography studio and library. The roof pitches slightly (Kameon conceived of it as a tilted canvas), dripping streams of color inspired by the abstract pour paintings of Helen Frankenthaler and Morris Louis of the 1960s, complementing the modernist architecture.

OPPOSITE LEFT: Cast-in-place concrete pavers lead to the front entrance. Planted joints allow rainfall to percolate and stormwater to stay on-site. Most of the ground plane in the landscape is permeable, with generous space dedicated to planting, expanses of gravel, and decomposed granite. OPPOSITE RIGHT: The green roof of the garage-turned-photography studio serves as a focal point seen from multiple locations on the property.

OPPOSITE: Texture was key to the planting design. Clumps of Canyon Prince wild rye (*Leymus condensatus* 'Canyon Prince'), Mediterranean spurge (*Euphorbia characias* ssp. *wulfenii*), and agave frame the pool deck beneath a canopy of the existing native oaks. BELOW: A landing, made of hand-seeded concrete with aggregate, connects to broad concrete steps leading to a blue stone fire pit terrace—the clients' favorite "room" in the house.

Building Biodiversity

The Garden after the Storm

DESIGNING FOR BEAUTY AND RESILIENCY IN THE FLORIDA KEYS

Project: Coccoloba Garden
Location: Islamorada, Florida
Size: 7 acres
Designer: Raymond Jungles

By the morning of September 10, 2017, Hurricane Irma had made landfall as a Category 4 storm in the Florida Keys, pummeling the island chain with winds upward of 130 miles per hour and an eight-foot storm surge. It was less than a year after the Coccoloba Garden had been planted. The vegetation had just begun to fill in and transform the seven-acre coastal property into a landscape teeming with local flora and fauna. The owners had recently celebrated a wedding in the flourishing subtropical landscape. A few weeks after the festivities, the hurricane toppled nearly all of the trees and shrubs and destabilized the shoreline.

The entry garden is elevated and animated by a circuitous crushed-shell driveway. The existing hammock was enhanced with understory shrubs and a grove of Bailey palms (*Copernicia baileyana*).

Natural Revitalization

The storm, reportedly one of the strongest and costliest hurricanes on record in the Atlantic basin, caused significant damage across the southeastern United States. Compared to other properties affected by the storm, the Coccoloba Garden recovered with remarkable speed, thriving again within six months. Raymond Jungles, landscape architect and longtime resident of southern Florida, attributes the site's recovery to the design's proliferation of native plants. "Down there, if you get a hurricane and if you're using the wrong plants, you have to replace them all," Jungles said. On the other hand, he added, "If you look at how the Florida Keys' natural vegetation survives after a hurricane, you can't even tell that there was a hurricane a year after because everything grows in these thick forests they call hammocks."

From the upland hardwood hammock to the intertidal mangroves and the coastal dunes, native plants in the Keys have adapted to frequent disturbances, like hurricanes, and help protect communities in the low-lying islands in extreme weather events. Southern Florida supports the only subtropical ecological community in the continental United States, with numerous endemic plant species and a range of regional vegetation, including temperate mainland species and tropical species from the Caribbean.

Hammocks are found throughout the Everglades ecosystems, and they consist of broad-leaf trees that grow with a dense canopy, providing the ideal filtered-light understory conditions for moisture-loving plants, like the native ferns of the Florida Keys. They exist at a slightly higher elevation, only a few inches, than the surrounding ecologies, including mangroves. Species that thrive in the wetlands are well adapted to brackish coastal conditions, where saltwater from the Atlantic Ocean meets freshwater in the Everglades, the channels and rivers that weave throughout southern Florida.

LEFT: Oolite lines the edges of cascading saltwater ponds on this coastal property. The landscape sustained significant damage in the wake of Hurricane Irma, but the native plant communities' natural revitalization process brought the garden back to life within six months. A specimen button mangrove (*Conocarpus erectus*) was relocated to this prominent location.
ABOVE: Before the property was redesigned by Raymond Jungles, it featured a linear sand road lined by rows of palm trees and bordered by dense native hammock.

A Living Landscape

The Coccoloba Garden includes all of these plant communities and serves as a thriving portrait of the resiliency of native habitats in the Keys. The garden expresses the region's unique ecological diversity with careful attention to the site's hydrology and elevation. Jungles selected and located plants based on a particular species' ability to thrive given exposure to salt water, which begins at the approach to the house.

The property is situated just off of the Overseas Highway, a historic roadway spanning the islands along the southernmost portion of US Route 1. Where the road meets the site, Jungles carefully choreographed a nearly eight-hundred-foot-long entryway that leads to the main house. Along this crushed-shell path, he crafted meadows at the periphery of the hammock. As the path winds around the hammock and mangrove wetlands, it dips and climbs with subtle changes in elevation to reveal views, through swaths of native grasses growing in the dunes, to the azure water beyond.

Jungles aspired to create as many habitats, vistas, and garden spaces as possible given the length of the entry sequence from the arrival on the historic Overseas Highway to the waterfront residence. Located on Islamorada, a series of six islands nestled between Miami and Key West in Monroe County, the garden sits on top of an ancient coral-reef network that stretches the length of the Keys, from the Gulf of Mexico and along the Atlantic coast north of Miami. The property was once a part of a commercial shrimp farm. When the client purchased the lot, a quarry from the operation carved into the native Florida keystone still dotted the landscape. (Florida keystone is the exposed limestone bedrock indigenous to the Keys that formed below sea level.)

OPPOSITE: An oolite path winds through the saltwater pond flanked by red mangrove (*Rhizophora mangle*). BELOW: Jungles expanded a series of existing pools (a remnant from the property's former life as a commercial shrimp operation) and added saltwater fish that thrive in this environment.

Jungles expanded the existing pond and created terraced rock ledges with the more common Miami-Dade County oolite limestone to celebrate the surrounding specimen red mangroves (*Rhizophora mangle*). Aquatic consultants stocked the pond with indigenous fish species that thrive in brackish water prone to tidal fluctuations. Bird species, such as herons and egrets, flourish as they forge around the edges of the pond.

A large oolite monolith was carved into a water trough, while others were carved into planters with Madagascar ocotillo (*Alluaudia procera*). Purple flowers from swaths of Mexican bush sage (*Salvia leucantha*) and grasses, like sand cordgrass (*Spartina bakeri*) and seaside goldenrod (*Solidago sempervirens*), flourish in the sandy soils.

The expanded saltwater network expresses a material connection to the site's geological history while creating space for a flourishing fish display that invites even more life into the garden. "It's so beautiful to have living creatures—you get the birds that will come and try to eat the fish. You create a mini-ecosystem," Jungles said. "We're into living gardens, not just gardens that look good. We want gardens that entertain with butterflies, birds, and creatures."

The design employs native plants to create a lush, resilient garden that supports the local habitat. In the hardwood hammock, the tallest trees, such as Bailey palms, cast dappled shade on an understory of native grasses and flowering ground covers.

LEFT: The design features both oolite and keystone, both of which are limestones that contain fossil imprints. The walls are planted with blooming aloe vera and baby rubber plant (*Peperomia obtusifolia*). BELOW: The retaining walls were constructed using oolite limestone.

ABOVE: "Dunes [offer] frontline protection," Jungles said. "A big storm surge could eat a dune away, but that's what it does, it stabilizes the grade." He used plants that grow naturally on dune systems, like sand cordgrass (*Spartina bakeri*), silver saw palmetto (*Serenoa repens* 'Cinerea'), spider-lily (*Hymenocallis latifolia*), and golden creeper (*Ernodea littoralis*).

OPPOSITE TOP: The veranda, accented by a Florida keystone border wall, affords views toward the pool and beachfront garden. OPPOSITE BOTTOM: The site required sophisticated drainage and grading. A series of retaining walls, paths, and planting gradually raise the landscape to meet the house, concealing the first floor, which is set on pillars to avoid flooding in storm events. The design creates "a sense that you're *in* the garden versus *over* it," Jungles said.

A Desert Vernacular

DESIGNING WITH WALLS, SHADOWS, AND NATIVE PLANTS

Project: Palo Cristi Garden
Location: Paradise Valley, Arizona
Size: 1.5 acres
Designer: Steve Martino Landscape Architect

Martino added ninety native trees to supplement the existing native trees along the driveway and throughout the site. He found inspiration for his planting strategy from the microclimates created by the canopy along the arroyo, a dry stream bed subject to seasonal flooding, which extends the wetness of the spring rain into the summer.

It was, in part, a political statement. "There was so much resistance to using native plants. I almost starved," Steve Martino said, explaining how he started using native plants at a time when the typical yard in the desert included pine trees and lawn. Martino, who has a background in architecture, is a fervent advocate for desert ecologies. "I was on a mission to bring the desert back into the city."

It was also a practical decision—native desert plants are drought tolerant and have adaptations to survive the harsh summers and the low temperatures of the fall and winter. In the 1970s, when Martino first started designing landscapes, local nurseries didn't carry native plants, so he began collecting seeds from the desert. He and a friend—Ron Gass, a horticulturalist and then a graduate student, who had received a grant from Lady Bird Johnson's highway-beautification program—would go on trips into the deserts of southern Arizona and northern Mexico to pick seeds and then experiment to see what would grow. If the seeds they collected grew successfully, Gass would sell them at his small, native plant nursery in Phoenix, and Martino would use them in his designs.

BELOW: The auto court is lined with native Sonoran Desert species like desert spoon (*Dasylirion wheeleri*) and century plant (*Agave americana*). OPPOSITE TOP: The lacy canopy of a native mesquite tree casts dappled shade over century plants set against the red-orange wall of the guest house. OPPOSITE BOTTOM: Ocotillo (*Fouquieria splendens*) with an electric blue wall beyond. Martino used native plants for their striking beauty as well as their ability to attract wildlife. "They bring their entourage with them, which I call pollinators and predators," Martino said. "You tap into the food chain, and then it becomes a habitat."

The Palo Cristi Garden

The property on Palo Cristi Street is a twenty-five-year-old example of Martino's distinctive design vernacular that celebrates arid landscapes, using the plants that homeowners had for years considered weeds. Martino calls the house a "modern hacienda" in a neighborhood of McMansions. The building is understated with concrete floors, glass on the north and south facades, and without windows on the east and west facades. Following a visit to Mexico, the clients contacted Martino. They were inspired by Luis Barragán and wanted a garden that captured the bold simplicity of the renowned architect's home in Mexico City.

When the clients bought the one-and-one-half-acre lot, it was an illegal dumping site for construction debris, littered with trash and chunks of asphalt and concrete. It had an arroyo running through it, also known as a wash, a naturally occurring, seasonally dry streambed lined with several mature native trees.

LEFT: Peruvian old man cactus (*Espostoa lanata*) and Mexican fence post cactus (*Lophocereus marginatus*) meet a wall as it intersects with the water feature.

Martino designed a long, gravel driveway, lined with palo verde and desert willow, that snakes alongside the arroyo until it reaches what he describes as an "auto court"—a sun-drenched courtyard with clusters of shrubs and cactuses lining the steps to the main entrance. Two gardens cap the north and south sides of the house, each with a long, trough-style water feature. Groups of native plants are situated along the building, under the dappled shade of the canopy, which Martino supplemented with ninety new native trees. The kitchen floor extends out to a covered terrace with views to the arroyo and the Tonto National Forest. Where the existing landscape had been disturbed, Martino used a seed mix to regenerate the native habitat.

Privacy, Color, and Shadow

The clients purchased the property assuming no one would buy the one adjacent to it, as it was nearly five feet lower than street level. However, eventually the property was sold, and the new owners installed a tennis court within view of the client's dining terrace. To block the views of the neighbors, Martino added a freestanding, eight-foot-tall fireplace against a warm, rust-colored stucco wall. He called it a "modern landscape folly." As the other lots in the subdivision sold, Martino continued to add walls and planting for privacy, likening the strategy to a game of chess— a move, then a countermove—to shield the understated, contemporary home from the surrounding development.

Ocotillo (*Fouquieria splendens*) against a lemon-colored wall. A stunning display of shadows is cast onto a corner of the house.

In addition to providing privacy, the fireplace functions as an integral design element, juxtaposing the muted, gray-green palette of the desert with pops of vibrant color painted on stucco walls. Rather than just displaying bursts of color seasonally when the cactuses bloom, the walls provide year-round visual interest. They also act as a canvas for a shifting display of shadows as the sun casts light through the planting and onto the wall, like a sun dial activating the space with movement and texture. "You need to think of the sun as a separate building material," Martino said. "It's so damn harsh, it can ruin something, or it can enhance it."

The Palo Cristi Garden relates to the larger landscape through the bold, uncomplicated beauty of native desert plants and the life they invite into the garden. Within the garden, the plants, set against colorful, monolithic walls, express an intrinsic connection between the delicate ecology of the desert, the arid climate, and the built environment.
To Martino, the native desert landscape is the "state-of-the-art evolution of place."

LEFT: A linear water feature with a bed of native planting beyond. Shrubs like desert spoon (*Dasylirion wheeleri*) and Caribbean agave (A*gave angustifolia* 'Marginata') are placed under a canopy of a mesquite tree (*Prosopis pubescens*).
OVERLEAF: The fireplace and wall screen views of the neighbor's property. Martino planted cactuses and shrubs in the front to activate the wall with shadows throughout the day.

A Wind-Swept Meadow above the Canopy

BUILDING URBAN HABITAT WITH GREEN ROOFS

Project: Greenwich Avenue
Location: New York, New York
Size: 3,500 square feet
Designer: Alive Structures

A naturalistic planting palette of wildflowers and shrubs weaves in color—
meadow sage (*Salvia nemorosa* 'Caradonna') for pops of purple, and white
gaura (*Gaura lindheimeri*) for dappled white hues—and creates a dynamic
meadow for this green roof high above Greenwich Avenue.

"Landscaping? What kind of landscaping do you do in New York City?" It has been a common reaction when Marni Majorelle discusses her work, particularly at the beginning of her career. She grew up in Brooklyn, where her mother was a landscape designer, and Majorelle worked for other local designers before starting her own company, Alive Structures, more than a decade ago to focus on building green roofs that use plants indigenous to the region. At the time, designing a green roof, let alone one using mostly native species, was still an abstract concept to many outside the field.

"In 2007, I had many challenges working with people in alignment with my vision, but then something interesting happened," she said. "The High Line opened." The High Line is a park built on a historic, elevated rail line on the western edge of Manhattan. The linear, one-and-half-mile-long pathway uses a mix of native and non-native perennials, grasses, and shrubs evocative of natural plant communities to create a dynamic yet approachable landscape. Majorelle attributes an interest among local clients in a more naturalistic beauty in part to the High Line.

A Dynamic, Urban Habitat

For a top-floor apartment with a 3,500-square-foot roof in the West Village, Majorelle created a garden that mirrors the curated wild of the High Line while capitalizing on the unique set of conditions afforded by an elevated landscape. Eight stories up, the garden floats above the canopy line where gusts of wind, unobstructed by trees, tousle swaths of grasses around mounding perennials and shrubs, creating a sense of movement and topographic relief amid an otherwise static horizon. The dynamic interplay of wind with the grasses around the perimeter of the roof animates the concrete pavers and trellis structure at the center. Large, potted trees cast dappled shade over areas for seating and entertainment, while a subdued palette of green to yellow hues, dotted intermittently with seasonal purples and pinks, enforces a sense of cohesion throughout the garden.

Apart from the grasses, Majorelle planted native species of wildflowers to create a rolling meadow layered with large shrubs and small trees for vertical interest. The project is an intensive green-roof system with up to two feet of engineered soil, which allows it to support a range of vegetation and helps to provide habitat for native birds, bees, and insects. New York City is a crucial stopover for migratory birds and butterflies along the East Coast. Central Park, with its extensive woodlands, meadows, and water systems, is particularly well suited for birds stopping over in the spring and fall. At the residential scale, too, green roofs can offer critical stopover opportunities for migratory species. "Even a green roof that doesn't have native plants hosts tons of different insects that are beneficials," Majorelle said, stressing the importance of maintenance practices that are mindful of all living creatures, like waiting until the spring to cut grasses back to sustain habitat throughout the winter.

LEFT: The planting buffers the edges of the roof around the seating and entertainment spaces. A dining area is protected by a shade structure and surrounded by concrete pavers. ABOVE: Majorelle aligns her maintenance practices to enable the garden to support habitat—in this case for migratory birds, bees, and insects. Rather than cutting back brown grasses in late fall, she said, "I cut grasses in late March. I think for aesthetic reasons as well as ecological reasons that's the right thing to do. It's also less work."

In addition to providing habitat, green roofs offer several environmental benefits, including capturing and retaining stormwater, which reduces the amount of pollution entering local ecosystems and helps to control flooding and erosion. Green roofs also cool the surrounding environment and contribute to reduction of the urban-heat-island effect, in which a temperature increase caused by hardscape surfaces in urban areas retains and radiates heat back to the environment. By lowering air temperatures, green roofs reduce air pollution and capture heavy metals that contribute to respiratory issues, like asthma. Green roofs can also limit a building's energy use by serving as a physical layer that both insulates and cools the structure.

The Layers of a Green Roof

The structure of a green roof varies by project, according to Majorelle. In many cases, she will first install a layer of waterproofing followed by a layer that serves as a barrier to protect the building from any aggressive root systems. On top of the root barrier is a drainage layer that consists of gravel or units of plastic plates, formed like an egg carton, with cups to retain water and holes to drain it, allowing oxygen to filter into the soil substrate. The next layer is fabric, which keeps the soil from escaping into the drainage layer. Above the fabric filter is the irrigation system. While not always required by a project, irrigation is often necessary to ensure that a green roof's thin soil profile does not dry out. Climate change, due to extreme weather patterns resulting in increasingly wet or hot weather, has made it even more difficult to completely remove irrigation from green roofs, noted Majorelle.

Green roofs have several ecological benefits, including stormwater management. "As our weather gets wetter with more dramatic storms, we need to have more sponges to capture more of that runoff. A hotter and wetter city really demands more green roofs, more vegetated spaces," Majorelle said.

The top layers of a green roof are the soil and plants. Because typical planting soil is biodegradable, green roofs use an engineered soil medium made from shale or slate that has been quarried and heated in a kiln to create tiny pieces of aggregate that do not break down like typical organic planting soil. While the engineered soil works well, creating it is an energy-intensive process. Still, it is a worthwhile trade-off in terms of sustainability, Majorelle said, given the long list of benefits green roofs provide. "I wouldn't do it if I didn't think the benefits were great," she said. "Green roofs have so many benefits. That's why I'm so committed to them."

BELOW: Purple hues of tall verbena (*Verbena bonariensis*) and Russian sage (*Perovskia atriplicifolia*) set against the bold, textural green of narrowleaf bluestar (*Amsonia hubrichtii*) are woven together in a mix of grasses. Green roofs can extend the life of a roof by protecting it from solar radiation and extreme weather. They can also increase the efficiency of rooftop mechanical equipment by lowering the air temperature.
OPPOSITE: Rattlesnake master (*Eryngium yuccifolium*) supports the naturalistic planting palette.

ABOVE: Swamp milkweed (*Asclepias incarnata*) mixed with Mexican feathergrass (*Nassella tenuissima*) provides a soft contrast against the New York skyline. RIGHT: Willow trees and vines creep over the shade structure at the center of the roof.

The Botanical Landscape

A SPECIMEN GARDEN IN THE CHAPARRAL

Project: Golden Oak
Location: Portola Valley, California
Size: 1.5 acres
Designer: Surfacedesign Inc.

The garden is perched on a hillside, adjacent to the house, with a patio facing east. From here, the property appears expansive, with long views that draw the eye across soft, rolling hillsides, peppered with oak woodlands, beyond the development of Silicon Valley, and out to the marbled turquoise blue of the San Francisco Bay. Just beyond the patio, chaparral shrubland descends into a dry riparian zone.

The site is a classic California landscape, notes designer Roderick Wyllie. While it enjoys the quintessential beauty of the region, it also faces a now-commonplace threat: fire. Located on a slope in the seasonally dry chaparral ecology, the property poses optimal conditions for the spread of wildfire.

Foxtail agave (*Agave attenuata*) and kangaroo paw (*Anigozanthos*) line a walkway of concrete pavers at the main entrance.

To mitigate the spread of fire and make space for the native landscape and wildlife, they cleaned up the existing landscape, cutting down brush and removing invasive species, such as poison oak and broom, often the worst for fire, to give the mature valley oaks sufficient space to thrive. Their intervention was more about "editing," Wyllie said. While his maintenance efforts in the back of the house would soon be imperceptible as the native landscape filled out, in the entry garden along the road, Wyllie envisioned a landscape entirely unique from its surroundings. The garden is unapologetically bold, profusely colorful, and rich in botanical curiosity, distinct from both the striking geometry of the architecture and the quietness of the native landscape, yet completely appropriate to the delicate ecological conditions around the property.

Color and Composition in the Garden

The property is in Portola Valley, a suburban enclave tucked into the middle of the south peninsula between the bay and the Pacific Ocean. Unlike many of the surrounding communities, Portola Valley has maintained its rural character, in part due to city-backed ecological guidelines that support the native landscape.

The clients also have a home in New Zealand, where they have the sort of lush, leafy garden afforded by the country's climate. Wyllie sought to create an immersive experience, expressive of the clients' adventurous, wandering spirits: "They love the idea of exuberance. They weren't shy about that."

While developing the design, he visited a botanical garden in Santa Cruz that captured, albeit less formally, the err of abundance and originality that he sought to bring to the project. "The garden [in Santa Cruz] is pretty ragtag; sometimes you don't know where the paths are and so you kind of get lost in it all," he said, admirably. "It has an amazing collection of plants."

Inspired, and aware that the typical meadow vernacular would have been too soft to be in conversation with the architecture, Wyllie designed a specimen garden around the house, contrasting vibrant color and horticultural novelty with the structure's monochromatic volumes. "The garden needed to have its own strength," he said.

OPPOSITE: Concrete pavers amble toward the main entrance. Beyond the walkway, the landscape descends rapidly into the chaparral. OVERLEAF: Through the careful composition of color and structure, designer Roderick Wyllie created an immersive experience with a specimen approach to plant selection and spacing.

At the entry, a curated selection of succulents, shrubs, and perennials line a concrete walkway that jogs from the motor court to an open portal at the main entrance. Plants were selected for their unique, sculptural character and saturated color, not only in terms of the flower but also the foliage. Meticulously placed specimens and groupings of plants coax visitors off the path, inviting the same impulse of spontaneous wandering as did the botanical garden in Santa Cruz.

Lime-green euphorbias and foxtail agaves (*Agave attenuata*), set in a field of warm, taffy-colored pea gravel, offset the cool turquoise century plant (*Agave americana*) and grayish blue concrete pavers and bench. Perennial groupings of fiery-red and yellow-tipped kangaroo paw (*Anigozanthos*) add height and texture below the canopy of a valley oak. A single tree aloe (*Aloe barberae*), set against the louvered facade, amplifies the garden's presence, its curious branching habit and vibrant leaves demanding attention against the architecture.

"To me, this is what a garden can do. It can certainly re-emphasize the architectural geometry, but in this case, what a garden can do, is totally and completely contrast the approach."

In each garden he designs, his style and approach adapt with hyper-local consideration to the existing conditions. Through unrestrained use of color and structure within an entirely unique composition, Golden Oak's relationship to the architecture is similar to how it relates to the surrounding native landscape. It is both a bold counterpoint and effortless complement to the presence of each, visually distinct yet appropriate to place.

Climate Change Is Changing Design

Each year, California's fire season lays bare the imperative to align the design of landscapes with the realities of a changing climate. In August of 2020, the coast side and mountains of Santa Cruz and San Mateo County, where Portola Valley is located, were struck by lightning, sparking a fire that burned over eighty-five thousand acres, marking the area's largest fire complex on record. In the wake of increasingly dramatic weather events, landscape designers are witnessing a shift as clients focus not only on the aesthetic of their landscapes but also on their resilience and performance within the local and regional environment. Wyllie attributes this shift, in part, to policy changes and political capital, but also to innovation on the part of the designers.

"I think that is our responsibility to make it something that's visually accessible to people," he said.

In the garden around the house, the specimen approach allows for a border of defensible space while still allowing for a contiguous relationship between the landscape and the architecture. The gravel creates critical fuel breaks, a non-combustible barrier that can slow the spread of wildfire, between groups of fire-resistant plants, such as succulents, with leaves that contain more moisture than native chaparral plants. Less fire-resistant vegetation, like meadow grasses, are pulled away from structures to mitigate the risk of ignition.

Wyllie didn't set out to create a garden focused on fire suppression. Though paradoxically, or perhaps intuitively, as a long-time designer in California, in approaching the design with the impulse to create space to wander, he established a spatial framework for fire suppression in a garden where botanical exuberance goes hand-in-hand with resiliency in landscape design.

OPPOSITE TOP: Delicate pastel-flowering perennials—white gaura (*Gaura lindheimeri*) and blue sea holly (*Eyrngium amethystinum*)—mix with meadow grasses, foothill stipa (*Stipa lepida*), blue grama (*Bouteloua gracilis*), and silky spike melic (*Melica ciliata*). The meadow replaced a lawn to reintegrate the garden with the native landscape. OPPOSITE BOTTOM: Naked coral tree (*Erythrina coralloides*) flowers above the meadow at the edge of the specimen garden. OVERLEAF: Instead of seamless groundcover, Wyllie chose a specimen approach to the layout of the garden. "Oftentimes, when you're thinking about bringing color into a space, you think about layering and you think about depth," he said, "But in this case, it is more about patches, with bursts of color."

OPPOSITE: In the front of the house, the garden consists of fire-resistant plants, like succulents and woody perennials, with ample space between groups of planting to create fuel breaks. More combustible vegetation, like the meadow grasses, are a safe distance from the house and other structures. ABOVE + OVERLEAF: A sun-drenched patio offers views through the rolling hillsides toward the San Francisco Bay. Beyond the patio, the landscape descends into a dry riparian zone with ample wildlife. Existing valley oaks (*Quercus lobata*) were supplemented with additional oak trees, while invasive species were removed, helping the existing native landscape to thrive.

Environmental Stewardship

Relating to the Land

AN EXPLORATION OF SOIL, COMPOSITION, AND FORM

Project: Franklin Farm
Location: Hampshire, England
Size: 35 acres
Designer: Kim Wilkie

At twilight, deep shadows are cast into a depression, an Archimedean spiral that has been sculpted into the rich chalk downs of Franklin Farm on England's southern coast. The spiral unwinds, crossing beneath a fence on the eastern side of the property and becoming a path mowed through a grazing pasture. As the path stretches across the meadow, it coils into a sculpted mound nestled at the edge of the woodlands. For landscape architect Kim Wilkie, the inverted spirals express a balance between the surface and soil, a harmonious relationship between a complex subterranean ecosystem and human engagement with its surface.

The Soil

The farm has been in Wilkie's family for decades. His grandfather heard about the homestead in 1962, when it was about to be demolished. His parents bought the ruin and made it habitable. Today, it's where Wilkie and his partner live, farm, and explore an approach to landscape design based in regenerative agriculture.

Wilkie's curiosity and engagement is evident throughout the thirty-five-acre site. In addition to the spiral earthworks, a serpentine ha-ha wall curves along the western side of the farm, dividing the property between the house, with its surrounding courtyards and barns, and the meadow. (A ha-ha is a landscape wall, typically sunken into the ground, that retains the land on either side to create a vertical barrier without interrupting a view.)

After Wilkie expanded the property by buying some of the farm's original fields, he set out to regenerate the plowed land, which had degraded over the years due to conventional farming. He built the ha-ha and created grazing meadows. He used manure from the cows and chickens combined with rotational grazing and haymaking to restore the biological life of the soil.

"You can't treat soil as chemical substrate. It is actually biological life," Wilkie noted. Cultivation practices over the last century of intensive farming have thinned the topsoil and degraded its organic matter, the nutrient-rich layer that is essential to the health of all ecosystems and to people's ability to grow food. The chalky soil at Franklin Farm, and all along England's Channel coast, is highly alkaline, making it fertile for both wildlife and wildflowers and an ideal natural composition for sculpting the earth. "I just love mud and sculpting things, and it really is a great place to do that," Wilkie said. Though the soil is essentially bedrock, it is very pliable, he added. "You can carve vertical slopes in it, and they will stay in place."

A flint wall, a ha-ha, holds back a field of wildflowers and grasses around the house.

Embedded in the bright, fine-grained chalk soil are shards of flint, a dark, crystalline deposit that is ubiquitous at Franklin Farm. Wilkie collected pieces of flint as he dug around the property and used it to build walls and paths that connect the gardens closest to the house, including the vegetable garden and orchard, as well as the cow barn and farmyard. He captures rainwater from the roofs and uses it to irrigate the vegetable and flower gardens.

The Dew Pond

Just beside the house and before the ha-ha and pasture is a dew pond. Because the soil, being chalk, is very porous, water runs through it quickly. Historically, Wilkie explained, to help with water retention on the surface and avoid erosion, farmers operating on chalk soils would pen sheep in an area for a week or so. Their hooves stomping on the ground and their urine would compact the soil into a cement-like, impervious layer able to contain water. Each day, the soil warms under the sun and then condenses into moisture as the air cools at night, so even when there is no rain, the ponds are self-replenishing.

Farmers in the desert use a similar technique, Wilkie noted, where the change of temperature of stones at the bottom of a shallow depression captures the moisture at night. "The most elegant example I've come across is when they plant things in the desert, they'll put a smooth pebble over the seed so that the water that condenses on the pebble runs down the sides, and waters the seed," he said.

Two Strands

In addition to farming, Wilkie is a designer known for his carefully articulated earthworks that make no effort to conceal the manipulation of nature by the human hand, as many landscape designs do. On the surface, his highly refined topography forms, juxtaposed with the more informal nature of a farm, appear at odds, but the two strands have developed in tandem over the years. Wilkie's artistic practice is inspired by a Celtic tradition of physical engagement with the earth, while his farming expresses a deep appreciation for its productive qualities—both acknowledge humans as an intrinsic part of the natural process. "The idea that ecology and our responsibility to the natural world is simply about scientific systems misses the point," he said. "It's about how we relate to the land."

LEFT: Chickens travel down a mowed path into the meadow, and a spiral mound animates one edge of the property. MIDDLE: A sculpture by artist Simon Thomas sits at the center of a sunken spiral, the inverse of the mound in the adjacent meadow. Designer Kim Wilkie experiments with the composition of the soil and earth form through regenerative agriculture and landscape design. RIGHT: Wilkie planted the dew pond to help clean and filter the water, creating an excellent habitat for frogs.

LEFT: A herd of longhorn cattle grazes in the pasture with the woodlands beyond. Over the years, Wilkie restored the native woodlands that line the edges of the property, planting more than four thousand trees. As the trees have matured, they act as windbreaks from the Channel. ABOVE: The property near England's Channel coast was passed down through Wilkie's family. As seen from above, the woodlands line the perimeter of the pasture and farm.

OPPOSITE: A cow grazes in the pasture beyond the ha-ha. "I think a more intimate connection between human beings, growing food, the countryside, and production… feels like quite a good recipe for the planet," Wilkie said. "You don't see wildlife as separate. It's got to be an entire part of how you live on the planet." BELOW: Chicken forage in the farmyard. Their manure is high in nitrogen and a rich source for fertilizer. LEFT: A vehicular path runs through the farmyard. The buildings and walls around the house create a series of contained courtyards and gardens.

A Landscape, Balanced

RESTRAINT AND MINIMALISM IN SOUTHERN CALIFORNIA

Project: Takashi
Location: Mar Vista, California
Size: 5,500 square feet
Designer: Terremoto

BELOW: **A ginkgo tree (*Ginkgo biloba*) in a bed of Lagunita wild rye (*Leymus triticoides* 'Lagunita'), with Mexican weeping bamboo (*Otatea acuminata*) beyond. Lagunita is both an evergreen, no-mow ground cover and an ideal, low-water alternative to the traditional lawn.**
OVERLEAF: **Totem pole cactus (*Lophocereus schottii* var. *monstrosus*) and century plant (*Agave americana*) pop against the matte-black facade of the house.**

The garden design grew from a conversation between friends. Landscape architect David Godshall did a sketch. Architect Takashi Yanai, the client, drew over it. Godshall sketched some more—a specimen tree here, screening there. Repeat.

Yanai and Godshall are friends and have collaborated on projects in Los Angeles for years. But this project was different. It was for Yanai and his family. What emerged from their sketches was a landscape that, in its rejection of the traditional suburban form, fit perfectly into the city's Westside neighborhood. It is a small-scale, low-tech, and low-carbon design, minimal and balanced. It connects the spirit and horticultural traditions of California and Japan with an unapologetically legible human hand.

The Pivot

The first thing Yanai did when he started renovations on his modest
home was to paint the house matte black. Once he had made this pivot
from the neighborhood vernacular, Yanai called Godshall to build
a landscape that matched it. "He builds these profoundly big, beautiful,
modernist ground-up homes," Godshall said of Yanai, and here he was,
living in traditional, twentieth-century "non-architecture" in Mar Vista,
a low-key, suburban community adjacent to Venice.

Godshall described the house's existing planting as "prototypically
postwar and ecologically nihilist." And although he approaches each
project with deep appreciation for its context and existing conditions,
this one was a nonstarter. "There was a magnolia tree and some shrubbery
of no significance" on the 5,500-square-foot lot, he said. They replaced
it all, save for a fence draped in vines, which provided a textural green
backdrop for the new landscape design.

Foothill needlegrass (*Nassella lepida*) flanks an entryway of concrete pavers.
The owner, architect Takashi Yanai, painted the house black—a dramatic backdrop
for verdant green planting.

Water Wise, No Mow

Similar to the way the house pivots away from the style of the neighborhood, the landscape subverts the monotony of the standard lawn with a water-wise, no-mow ground cover. The grass is *Leymus triticoides* 'Lagunita', a drought-tolerant selection of creeping wild rye found by horticulturist and nurseryman John Greenlee. Greenlee is an ornamental-grass aficionado. He came across the native clone in the mid-1990s on a ranch near Santa Cruz and began propagating it after a massive drought left Californians questioning the logic behind their thirsty lawn-heavy yards.

Leymus triticoides 'Lagunita' is a sod-forming, evergreen grass. Godshall planted it in a sea of gray pea gravel that surrounds the house, and it grows in dense waves of green. It flows over a berm, "a spatial foil," to otherwise rectilinear garden forms, where Yanai's kids play. It doesn't need much, if any, water; it rarely flowers or seeds; and it's shorter than its native cousin, making it a tidy alternative to the English lawn.

The design weaves together Californian and Japanese aesthetics through subtle gestures in form and plant selection. Beyond the deck, an existing fence covered in climbing fig (*Ficus pumila*) serves as a green backdrop to a berm of Lagunita wild rye (*Leymus triticoides* 'Lagunita'). Bamboo adds a secondary layer of screening.

The Balance

In the front yard, the silvery-blue foliage of an acacia screens outside views into the house, while bamboo provides privacy from the street. In between, Yanai built a bench out of reclaimed wood and inexpensive, off-the-shelf concrete bases from the hardware store. The family now sits there in the morning, waving hello to neighbors.

At the back of the house, gravel disappears under a floating deck and anchors a specimen palo verde that casts an intricate web of shade over the custom-made Corten steel firepit. Bamboo lines the perimeter of the property, providing privacy and concealing a set of support cables attached to an outside utility pole that happens to jut into the yard. "One of those weird, life-in-the-city things," Godshall laughed.

Unlike the grass and palo verde, the acacia and bamboo planting need irrigation—and that's fine. The acacia and bamboo are strategic insertions, part of a larger conversation balancing the family's Californian and Japanese heritages. "I'm okay building a meaningful space for a family that's going to use an appropriate amount of water," Godshall said.

BELOW: The bench is made from inexpensive concrete bases from a local hardware store and custom-cut reclaimed wood from Angel City Lumber, a Los Angeles–based company that repurposes fallen trees throughout the city. OPPOSITE BOTTOM: Timber stumps are artfully sawn by wood sculptor Ido Yoshimoto. The deck is made from Ipe, a tropical hardwood that is difficult to source sustainably, but widely used in landscape design. Looking back, Godshall said he would have considered alternatives like Robi decking—black locust (*Robinia pseudoacacia*) lumber grown in the United States that behaves like a hardwood in its durability and resistance to rot.

ABOVE: A palo verde (*Parkinsonia florida* 'Desert Museum') and Corten steel firepit surrounded by pea gravel in the back of the house. LEFT: Sometimes, where the ecological argument can lose people, beauty makes the case for a deeper connection. "If you can prove to people that a native and/ or regionally appropriate garden can also just be really awesome and fun and beautiful, that's how you really win," Godshall said.

A Bold and Evolving Vignette

PLANTING IN COMMUNITIES FOR BEAUTY AND LONGEVITY

Project: Jones Road
Location: Girard, Illinois
Size: 0.5 acres
Designer: Adam Woodruff

It's been more than a decade since Adam Woodruff first planted the garden, enveloping a single-family home outside a rural community, thirty miles southwest of Springfield, in the heart of Illinois. "It started in 2008, and it's a work in progress," Woodruff said. Each time he visits, he revises, adds, and augments the planting, allowing the design to evolve over time.

The twenty-thousand-square-foot garden, set against the muted tan and green hues of the rolling woodlands that surround the property, is a vivid abstraction of a meadow. It is reminiscent of a native prairie in composition but with dramatic bursts of color and texture in the spring and summer, followed by the crisp, bronzed patina of leaves in the fall and the stark structure of branches in the winter. It was one of his earliest large-scale residential projects as a landscape designer, and even as it continues to change, the garden remains a poignant illustration of the emotive power of plants.

The Borrowed View

Prior to the design, the landscape around the house was minimal, consisting of a concrete patio with a pool and waterslide surrounded by lawn. After spending some time on the property, Woodruff determined that the site was off balance both visually and topographically.

The house sits on a ridgeline and the landscape beyond the pool deck took a steep pitch downward, limiting the level area for planting and stunting the garden within the greater landscape. Beyond the slope, a native meadow and woodland unfolded in the distance. That view, Woodruff explained, needed to become a part of the garden. He used soil from the site to level the slope and located a planting bed, approximately twenty feet from the house and outside of the immediate planting area around the pool, to create a long view across the property that blended the garden with the native landscape.

A tapestry of herbaceous and woody plants blends the vivid garden into the distant native landscape. The garden is contained and orderly near the house and slowly dissolves as it reaches toward the woodlands.

Planting for Beauty and Longevity

Initially, Woodruff explained, he took more of a block-style approach to planting, with a specific area for each species. For example, "an area that was full of *Sporobolus* with some *Echinacea* coming up or a swath of *Calamagrostis* to stop the eye and then in front of that *Veronicastrum*. It was more distinct, blocky plantings."

Over the years, however, as Woodruff traveled and experimented with planting strategies, the aesthetic at Jones Road shifted to a more intermingled style in which planting is organized in soft drifts of mixed perennials and grasses. The key to a successful, long-lasting garden, Woodruff said, is the right plant palette, and the key to developing a successful plant palette is thinking about the plants' associations to one other.

Woodruff created planting beds on the newly level area and down the slope to visually expand the garden into its surroundings.

He designs "a plant community not based on necessarily the native associations but the cultural requirements of the plant." The sun, moisture, and water requirements as well as the soil are the basic elements too often overlooked in favor of personal plant preference when developing a palette. Woodruff is not a native plant purist—about 30 percent of the plants at Jones Road are native or native cultivars. He selects plants based on their suitability to the climate and site attributes and on how a plant works with other plants in the garden.

In terms of aesthetics, Woodruff designs in layers and vignettes, considering first the structural elements, the upper layer of trees and shrubs. In a meadow garden like Jones Road, larger, more robust perennials and grasses serve as the structural layer, helping to balance the overall garden composition with the middle, more seasonal layer of perennials and lower grasses, and finally, the lower, ground-cover layer.

The garden celebrates the emotive qualities of plants. Woodruff used a mixture of tall, structural grasses with a mid-layer of seasonal perennials. A patinaed sculpture adds vertical interest to the composition.

Maintaining Beauty and Longevity

Shortly after he started Jones Road, he took a trip to Hummelo, in the
Netherlands, to visit renowned landscape designer Piet Oudolf and
tour his private garden. Oudolf is a master gardener, known for creating
captivating, romantic swaths of perennials and grasses. He is now
Woodruff's mentor and friend. His initial visit to Oudolf's property was
an almost spiritual experience and formative in terms of his career. "It was
an awakening. I realized the power of the plants to create atmosphere
and stir emotion." When Woodruff came home, he started to think about
his work in a different way.

Woodruff's Jones Road client approached him after admiring his
work at their bank in Springfield. In this commercial project, Woodruff
used approximately 180 species of plants, 40 percent of which were
annuals, in a design that required a skilled horticulturalist and dedicated
weekly maintenance regime. At Jones Road, Woodruff sought to create
a dynamic, perennial garden, both sophisticated in composition and one
that could sustain lasting beauty without extensive intervention once
the planting was established.

"[The clients] continue to invest in this garden because it's not static.
It is a garden that's right on the edge of being wild," Woodruff said. "As a
designer, I think it's our job to make sure the client understands the long-
term implications of their choices. If you want an annual garden, you want
to make sure you have the right person designing and installing it every
year because that's a tall order for it to be successful."

ABOVE: Prairie grasses provide a golden backdrop to leafy
perennials in the foreground. Now established, the garden
requires little supplementary water in part due to the
designer's selection of plants like *Sporobolus*, wild indigo
(*Baptisia*), and *Silphium* with deep root systems that help
them survive in drought-like situations. LEFT: The garden
becomes luminous as the plants catch the low, afternoon light.
OVERLEAF: A bronze sculpture by Ohio-based artist Thomas
Yano draws the eye across the garden, through the mounding
perennials and textural grasses.

The Balance

There is a tension, a delicate push and pull, between designing for beauty and sustaining it. Maintenance often comes down to a cost-benefit analysis between a plant's visual qualities and its behavior in a garden. Take, for example, rattlesnake master (*Eryngium yuccifolium*) and prairie dock (*Silphium terebinthinaceum*), both heavy reseeders that Woodruff approaches in different ways.

Woodruff lived in St. Louis, Missouri, when he worked on Jones Road and made regular trips back to the property after the project was complete to help maintain the garden. He has since relocated to the East Coast but makes regular trips back to check on the garden and to adjust the density of certain plants, as some naturally spread and can dominate the palette. As he returned year after year, rattlesnake master had reseeded so heavily that Woodruff removed it, though seedlings continue to pop up. Prairie dock, on the other hand, had also reseeded itself throughout the garden but, Woodruff explained, the role it serves in terms of aesthetics—its tall stems capped with sunny pops of yellow reaching above the mid-perennial layer—far outweighs a few hours of maintenance thinning out the plant each year.

ABOVE: The garden maintains its distinctive character throughout the seasons. Autumn hues warm the garden in late fall. LEFT: Purple coneflower (*Echinacea purpurea* 'Rubinstern') and narrowleaf mountain mint (*Pycnanthemum tenuifolium*).

LEFT: The garden in the fall. Smokebush (*Cotinus coggygria* 'Royal Purple') mixed with moor grass (*Molinia arundinacea* 'Skyracer'), little bluestem (*Schizachyrium scoparium* 'The Blues'), lamb's ear (*Stachys byzantina*), and others. BELOW: Matrix planting uses a limited number of species, approximately six to seven, arranged by percentage, or ratio of planting, in each area. OPPOSITE: Hues of purple and red dot the garden around the stone patio. "Nature and native plant communities inspire me. I like to blend plants in new ways. My work is about creating beauty and evoking an emotional response," Woodruff said.

When to Do Nothing

EVOLUTION AND ADAPTATION IN THE GARDEN

Projects: Margie Ruddick's Gardens
Locations: Pennsylvania and New York
Size: Various
Designer: Margie Ruddick Landscape

A s a well-established landscape architect, Margie Ruddick has devoted meticulous attention to the seemingly imperceptible details that make human-designed outdoor spaces feel dynamic and appear natural, flourishing as if they had always been there.

As a homeowner, she had no interest in a deep level of engagement with her landscape. There was the pressure of perfecting the placement of every stone paver, the patience and research needed to compose a thriving plant palette, and, of course, the time commitment required to maintain such a space. It was all too much for a business owner and mother, and yet, as she would later learn, she at least had to do something.

At her home in the East Mount Airy neighborhood of Philadelphia, designer Margie Ruddick let the landscape run wild. It slowly evolved into a now-cherished woodland garden, with places carved out for sitting and paths mown through swaths of grass.

Over the course of twenty years, Ruddick's identity as a gardener has evolved from inattentive suburban homeowner to misunderstood native plant activist to defiantly understated steward of the land. Her own gardens became spaces for an evolving and intentional practice in learning how, and where, to let go, balancing the natural process with the human experience.

OPPOSITE: The house in Sleepy Hollow was too close to her neighbors for another wild garden. Instead, she planted a series of magnolias and a holly tree (*Ilex*) and installed two areas for outdoor living, each with concrete pavers floated in a bed of large gravel. She kept the casual vibe of her garden in Philadelphia through the furniture—faux wicker chairs and tables that she bought online and painted a blueish silver to look like galvanized steel. BELOW: For her garden in Philadelphia, she designed a small seating area flanked by lawn and surrounded by native woodland species like swamp white oaks (*Quercus bicolor*), scarlet oaks (*Quercus coccinea*), mulberry (*Morus alba*), and multiflora rose that had seeded in over time.

Letting Nature Take Its Course

In 2004, Ruddick moved her family into a 1948 ranch, "a complete wreck of a house," in her words, on a third of an acre in Philadelphia's East Mount Airy neighborhood. She promptly gutted it, creating an open floor plan with massive windows that overlooked the backyard.

When it came to the garden, however, Ruddick ran out of steam. Initially, she simply mowed the lawn, as she despaired of what she should do with the land. She soon transitioned to mowing only the areas that would be useful as lawn: a small yard behind the house and the two paths that ran along either side of the house. She also located a small vegetable patch in her front yard. The rest, she let go.

As volunteer species—plants that were not intentionally planted—took over the unmown areas, her property quickly began to look a little unkempt, Ruddick admitted, and it became quite messy in the second year and downright unattractive in the third. Black cherries cropped up first; next, swamp white oaks and scarlet oaks seeded in; later, mulberry and multiflora rose appeared. It was the beginnings of a scrappy urban forest. By year six, the native tree species nearly reached the height of the roof of the house. She counted fourteen oak trees and one weeping cherry, a trophy plant she had dissuaded her own clients from purchasing. The appearance of this determined weeping cherry, right beside her driveway, struck her as sort of horticultural karma.

Ruddick's enthusiasm for her little forest restoration project was not shared by others.

"Strangers would come up and look in the windows, thinking that the house was abandoned," she said. Her preteen children were mortified, and at least one neighbor was incensed enough to report her to the building department for failing to comply with a municipal code requiring property owners to keep their front yards free of weeds over ten inches high. Ruddick soon received a summons for her "weedy," untamed yard. She appeared before the court, explaining that the "weeds" were saplings of white oak (*Quercus alba*), black cherry (*Prunus serotina*), and other native tree species, along with tall native milkweed that had taken over the patch of kale, rhubarb, marigolds, and zinnias she had planted.

In 2011, gardening columnist Anne Raver wrote a story about the incident for the *New York Times*, in which she described how an accomplished landscape designer's ecological gardening practices landed her in court. The "weed judge," in Ruddick words, dismissed the case, but to appease her neighbors, she started planting with more intention underneath the successional species, mostly asters, Virginia creeper (*Parthenocissus quinquefolia*), hellebores, and anemones. After the civic ordeal, she developed a new mowing plan to create lawn borders around the successional zones, creating what landscape architect and ecological designer Joan Nassauer called a "manicured margin" in her 1995 essay, "Messy Ecosystems, Orderly Frames." The clearly maintained lawn frames "convey a clear human intention to the 'wildness'" of the garden, explained Ruddick, who counts Nassauer among her influences.

As the garden grew, Ruddick continued to experiment. Her leaf and kitchen compost piles enhanced the soils around new plantings of shady perennials; her brush pile became home to a family of possums, who would emerge at night to drink from the large iron bowls she had repurposed as water gardens. By the time Raver's article appeared, Ruddick's wild garden had matured, and, suddenly, it felt truly alive. "By year seven, I wanted to be outside all the time," Ruddick said. "Some people say it takes a farm seven years to transition from chemical treatments to organic farming, for the chemicals to work their way out of the soil. It just kind of felt different, so I really do think there is a magic number."

OPPOSITE: **When Ruddick moved out of her house in Philadelphia she wondered if the next owners would embrace the wild garden as she had over the years. Much to the realtor's surprise, the house with the wild forest garden sold quickly to a couple who continued to care lovingly for the native landscape.**

The Gardner Grows

Ruddick's resolve to avoid designing her own garden was again tested when she left Philadelphia to move to a semidetached house in Sleepy Hollow, a walkable town in New York's Hudson Valley. Her new, compact neighborhood was full of gardeners who had planted a profusion of ornamental trees, shrubs, and perennials, warmed up with blasts of tropical annuals. Wild gardening was not an option.

"People live in close quarters," she said. "The mess involved in weed gardening would have been a blot on this beautiful block." Instead, she planted a series of magnolias, a large southern magnolia (*Magnolia grandiflora*) and a smaller saucer magnolia (*Magnolia x soulangiana*) in the backyard, and another delicate saucer magnolia along with a multistemmed holly tree in the front yard. Now self-aware and accepting of her laissez-faire tendencies as a gardener, she planted the understory with drought-tolerant species like strawberries and *Heuchera* and left the rest of the landscape bare to see what would crop up on its own. The specimen trees add structure to the landscape, while the lower species carry the spirit of her original gardening experiment in Philadelphia by allowing volunteer species to populate the understory. "In terms of trees, I have gone 'garden,' and the ground plane has kept my weed gardening instincts alive," she said.

Nature's Way

The third time Ruddick begrudgingly took on the design of a garden for herself occurred in the Hamptons, where she co-owns a house originally bought by her parents, in 1957, when it was a small shack on the beach. As a child, Ruddick played in the dunes, where Virginia creeper and stunted shrubs like bayberry (*Myrica pensylvanica*) edged the sand. Today, the existing landscape remains wild and scrubby, peppered with pines, scrub oaks, bayberry, and beach plum (*Prunus maritima*) that weave through a grid of dirt roads and quarter-acre lots originally developed in the 1920s.

OPPOSITE: Ruddick left the ground plane bare, inviting volunteers like morning glory (*Ipomoea*), wisteria (*Wisteria sinensis*), mulberry (*Morus alba*), Virginia creeper (*Parthenocissus quinquefolia*), and trumpet vine (*Campsis radicans*), which had grown over the fence from her neighbor's garden, to weave into her landscape.

Ruddick shares the property with a close-knit group of family and friends, who also grew up spending summers in the area. In 2017, following years of deferred maintenance, the group decided to renovate the house and surrounding landscape. After her usual hesitation, and with the added pressure of a shared home, Ruddick relented and set out to create a landscape that balanced the needs of multiple families and future generations with the delicate conditions of the coastal ecology. The house is located at the far eastern edge of Long Island at the point where the landscape dips down to coastal wash, and the vernacular is distinctly less manicured than is now common elsewhere in the Hamptons. The house and garden are nestled into the back dune, located away from the shoreline, and slightly below the primary dune closest to the water, where swaths of beach grass, dotted with beach pea (*Lathyrus japonica*), goldenrod (*Solidago*), and other flowering plants can be found. Planting in such ephemeral conditions is challenging given the limited number of species that can survive despite the constant spray of salty wind and nutrient poor sand.

"I have lived in this house since I was a baby, and this is my native landscape," Ruddick said. "I know what will grow here, which is not much, and what won't—most plants." Over the years, bayberry, beach plum, and scrub oak have grown in, as well as black pines, native to Japan, that have naturalized in this area. Reluctant to introduce a formal design language that would break with the native palette and organic flows of beachside volunteers, Ruddick contained her intervention to the areas closest to the house, planting mostly native species, including more bayberry and cedar, as well as some noninvasive species that can withstand the harsh environment, like creeping wire vine (*Muehlenbeckia axillaris*) and Adam's needle (*Yucca filamentosa*), which would not be found in this environment naturally.

In terms of function, her co-owners wanted a place that felt domesticated, particularly the kitchen garden. She established a language of warm gray stone pavers with gravel gaps and overlapping ground cover to define functional living spaces in the landscape: an outdoor kitchen, a side garden with outdoor shower, the "surf shop," where they store surf boards, and the front scrub meadows that separate the house from the road.

Over time, the beach house garden and its patrons have grown together. When New York shut down during the COVID-19 pandemic, the close-knit group spent ample time there together, working alongside one another in the recently established outdoor rooms and patio spaces, exceptionally grateful to spend time in a garden amid the lockdown.

Within a few years, the plants Ruddick installed started to soften, dissolving her design back into a landscape that has come to inform her identity as a gardener. Despite her initial resistance, Ruddick admitted to loving the way the volunteer species have mixed with the tiny leaves of the creeping wire vine she planted to fill in the joints and cracks between the pavers.

As with the garden in Philadelphia, she describes the amount of time it takes for a landscape to truly settled in as its magic number—when saplings have matured, shrubs have become a mosaic, grasses have unfurled, and signs of the human hand that planted the trees disappear and the landscape feels "natural," as if it has always been there.

"The most important thing for all of these landscapes," Ruddick said, referring to her gardens in Philadelphia, Sleepy Hollow, and the Hamptons, "is time." Be patient and curious, she added: "Tread lightly, edit, amplify and enhance, as opposed to doing everything from scratch."

The beach house has been in Ruddick's family since her parents bought it in the 1950s. Her father built a deck on the dune overlooking the ocean and another outside the living room. Throughout her childhood, she and her family lived outside all summer.

OPPOSITE + LEFT: **Concrete pavers form a pathway Ruddick laid out to designate outdoor spaces in the newly planted garden.**

BELOW + PREVIOUS BOTTOM: Pines, oaks, bayberry (*Myrica pensylvanica*), and beach plum (*Prunus maritima*) along with beachgrass (*Ammophila breviligulata*), dotted with beach pea (*Lathyrus japonicus*), and goldenrod (*Solidago*) grow in the dunes lining the boardwalk that leads to an ocean view. The Japanese black pines (*Pinus thunbergii*), which have become naturalized as the predominant tree species in the area and grow in the dunes, periodically fall victim to the black turpentine beetle. "It is a constantly changing and shifting landscape that corresponds to the ephemeral nature of the dunes themselves," Ruddick said.

The Vertical Landscape

THE IMPACT OF PLANTING IN A SMALL SPACE

Project: Lambolle Road
Location: London, England
Size: 1,700 square feet
Designer: Tapestry Vertical Gardens

In 2015, designer Adam Shepherd had just finished creating a large family garden in Belsize Park, in northwest London. Little did he know that a next-door neighbor and her children had watched from their first-floor window as he built the garden from scratch. Fast-forward five years, and the same neighbor invited Shepherd to design a green wall for the small patio in the back of the house she'd bought just down the road from her former neighbor. She told him that they had enjoyed watching him work, and searched for him online when they had bought their new house on Lambolle Road. As luck would have it, Shepherd had since transitioned to exclusively designing green walls.

At Lambolle Road, the green wall stretches across one side of a cedar fence that encloses the garden. The slats run horizontally, framing the swaths of planting from above and below. As they grow, the plants reach out into the garden, twisting together to form waves of texture and color.

Shepherd coordinated the plant species of the green wall with the garden on the ground, designed by John Davies, a London-based designer, to create continuity between the horizontal and vertical planes. Species like cranesbill (*Geranium* 'Rozanne') sweep purple hues across the wall and spill out onto the garden floor.

The Modular System

Shepherd created his first green wall in 2009 as part of a roof garden for an advertising agency in east London. There, he planted a triangular-shaped green wall on the gable end of the adjoining building. Since then, he has tried to incorporate green walls into every project.

The system he uses has stayed largely the same, building out the wall in modular panels, which he can edit down to a smaller size, or build up, clipping them together, like a jigsaw puzzle, to fill a vertical space. The panels consist of two layers of fabric, which are stapled to a recycled plastic panel. He cuts into the top layer of fabric, creating pockets into which the plants are inserted. He designs and builds the panels at his nursery in Devon, where he stores them for eight to twelve weeks to monitor the plants' progress, ensuring their health as they grow into the vertical system.

The green wall in the garden on Lambolle Road spans the full width of the garden, adding color and texture to the compact urban space.

He fastens the panels to a subframe, which is installed on site. The panel design has remained largely the same since his first project, in which he attached the living wall panels onto a stainless-steel framework. However, now, as a part of his continued desire to be more environmentally minded, he constructs the frames using a plastic wood lumber formed from 100-percent recycled plastics, collected from all over the United Kingdom.

The systems are soilless, which means that while there is soil in the root ball of the plant, no additional soil is added to the pockets. The plants are fed through a hydroponic system. The water flows from the top of the wall down, and excess is shed off the bottom into a drain that is either recycled back into the wall or, as is the case at Lambolle Road, into a soakaway, a drainage system for runoff, that collects water to irrigate the garden on the ground.

Plant Selection

"Once you've created a few vertical gardens, you start to know how the plants move or interact with each other," Shepherd said. "Like any garden, you'll start with the criteria that will guide your selection, such as the orientation of the wall or if a location is particularly windy, and then you'll know which plants will thrive in a vertical way."

Plants like hydrangeas grow well on the vertical plane, Shepherd said, adding that some plants, as they begin to grow out and away from the wall, will start to crumble under their own weight, then become strong and begin to rise again. After a few years, some plants, like fuchsia, get more muscular and have a more compelling presence when planted on a green wall. "In my opinion," Shepherd noted, "when planted at ground level, fuchsia is relatively unremarkable, but if you plant it in a living wall, above head height, the branches reach out into space and the flowers hang like teardrops, or pearls."

OPPOSITE: The house opens to the garden. The green wall provides a verdant green backdrop to the interior. BELOW: Designer Adam Shepherd coordinated the plant species of the green wall with the rest of the garden to create continuity between the horizontal and vertical planes. Purple geraniums sweep across the wall and in the garden on the ground.

The Power of Plants

Green walls have ecological and sustainability benefits, particularly in cities, by reducing stormwater runoff and helping to mitigate the urban-heat-island effect. Using the right plants, green walls can also support habitat and increase biodiversity. Shepherd's work focuses on the psychological impact planting can have at a small, urban scale. Increasingly, he has received inquiries from clients about creating a green wall that is the whole garden. In a compact, urban context, vertical planting saves precious occupiable space and shifts the focus from the ground to plants growing at eye level.

"If you were to have maybe six square meters [sixty-five square feet] of planting on the ground, and you took those six square meters of planting and put them on the wall, the power that has is quite amazing because the plants are coming at you. They're at the same height as you. They sit at eye level and almost crash over you like a wave," Shepherd said. He believes that "there is a very recognizable benefit to people's state of mind. It's hard to prove with science, but it's something we feel as human beings—if you can interface with greenery, it's going to make you feel better."

LEFT + OVERLEAF: **The garden softens the edges of the small, urban yard.**

Acknowledgments

My deepest gratitude goes to the designers of these beautiful gardens and to the clients and spaces that inspired them. Thank you for sharing your stories and expertise with me. I am deeply honored to have had the opportunity to explore the designs with such depth and engagement. A special thanks to Timothy Schuler for a profoundly thoughtful and eloquent introduction to this collection of work. This book would not have been possible without Jared Green, an invaluable mentor and friend, whose belief in my work set this project in motion. Thank you for your endless guidance and friendship.

To my parents, Ann and Steve Davidsen, for your unwavering support and generosity. Thank you for your thoughtful insights and for encouraging my passions with such enthusiasm. To my friends, a countless many of whom I have been in dialogue with for years as I wrote this book, especially Mark Wessels, Greta Mayne, Cate Capsalis, Heidi Loosen, and my cousin Alice Arnold, for your patience and humor. To my fellow graduate students and professors at the University of California, Berkeley, you have been a constant source of inspiration and knowledge as I have grown within the field of landscape architecture.

Thank you all for believing in me. Writing this book has been a unique privilege, and I am endlessly appreciative of your support.

Dana Davidsen is a landscape designer and writer based in the San Francisco Bay Area. She has written for a variety of publications on topics ranging from the environment to politics and holds an MA in landscape architecture from the University of California, Berkeley.

Photography Credits

Front Cover: Stephen Dunn
Back Cover (top to bottom):
Steve Martino, Kim Wilkie,
Adam Shepherd
2–3: Larry Weaner

Introduction
8: Charles Mayer
15: Adam Woodruff

Engaging Natural Systems
16–23: Meghan Montgomery
24: Kevin Scott
25–28: Meghan Montgomery
29: Berger Partnership
30–33: Kevin Scott
34–35: Madeleine Aguilar
36: Kate Russell
37: Surroundings Studio
38–39: Madeleine Aguilar
40: Narrative Media
41: Kate Russell
42–43: Sunny Khalsa
44: Kate Russell
46–47: Mikyoung Kim
48: Charles Mayer
49: Mikyoung Kim
50–54: Charles Mayer
55: Mikyoung Kim
56–61: Holly Lepere
62: Dawn Close
63–65: Holly Lepere
66–69: Andrew Montgomery
70–72: Nicole Brown
73: Andrew Montgomery
75: Nicole Brown

Restoration and Conservation
76: Larry Weaner
78–79: Lauren Stimson
80–83: Jon Levitt
84: Lauren Stimson
85–89: Jon Levitt
91–99: Larry Weaner
100–107: Marion Brenner
107 (bottom): Ron Lutsko
109: Mark Mahaney
110: Judy Kameon
111–113: Mark Mahaney
114: Erik Otsea
116–117: Mark Mahaney

Building Biodiversity
118: Marion Brenner
120–122: Stephen Dunn
123: Raymond Jungles
124–129: Stephen Dunn
130–141: Steve Martino
142–151: Marni Marjorelle
152–163: Marion Brenner
164–165: Paul Dyer

Environmental Stewardship
166: Adam Woodruff
168–175: Kim Wilkie
176–185: Stephen Schauer
186–197: Adam Woodruff
199–211: Margie Ruddick
212–219: Adam Shepherd
222–223: Adam Woodruff

Published by
Princeton Architectural Press
70 West 36th Street
New York, NY 10018
www.papress.com

ISBN 978-1-61689-907-3

Production Editor: Kristen Hewitt
Designers: Paul Wagner and Natalie Snodgrass

Library of Congress Control Number: 2021948966